Introducing Bruner

Sandra Smidt takes the reader on a journey through the key concepts of Jerome Bruner, a significant figure in the field of education whose work has spanned almost a century. His wide-ranging and innovative principles of early learning and teaching are unpicked here using everyday language and the links between his ideas and those of other key thinkers of the twentieth and twenty-first centuries are revealed.

Introducing Bruner is the companion volume to *Introducing Vygotsky*. The introduction of Bruner's key concepts is followed by discussion of the implications of these for teaching and learning. This accessible text is illustrated throughout with examples drawn from real-life early years settings, and the concepts discussed include:

- how children acquire language;
- how children come to make sense of their world through narrative;
- the significance of play to learning;
- the importance of culture and context;
- the role of memory;
- what children should be taught: the spiral curriculum;
- how children should be taught: scaffolding and interaction.

The book also looks, crucially, at what those working or involved with young children can learn from Bruner and includes a helpful glossary of terminology. This fascinating insight into the life and work of a key figure in early years education is essential reading for anyone concerned with the learning and development of young children.

Sandra Smidt is a writer and consultant in early years education. Her most recent books include: *Playing to Learn* (2010); *Planning for the Early Years Foundation Stage* (2009); *Key Issues in Early Years Education*, 2nd edn (as editor) (2009); *Introducing Vygotsky* (2008); *Supporting Multilingual Learners in the Early Years* (2007) and *A Guide to Early Years Practice*, 3rd edn (2007) – all published by Routledge.

Introducing Bruner

A guide for practitioners and students
in early years education

Sandra Smidt

Routledge
Taylor & Francis Group

LONDON AND NEW YORK

Published 2011
by Routledge
2 Park Square, Milton Park, Abingdon, Oxon OX14 4RN

Simultaneously published in the USA and Canada
by Routledge
270 Madison Avenue, New York, NY 10016

Routledge is an imprint of the Taylor & Francis Group, an informa business

Typeset in Garamond by Taylor & Francis Books
Printed and bound in Great Britain by CPI Antony Rowe, Chippenham, Wiltshire

British Library Cataloguing in Publication Data
A catalogue record for this book is available from the British Library

Library of Congress Cataloging in Publication Data
Smidt, Sandra, 1943-
   Introducing Bruner : a guide for practitioners and students in early years education / Sandra Smidt.
      p. cm.
   1. Bruner, Jerome S. (Jerome Seymour) 2. Early childhood education. I. Title.
   LB885.B792S65 2011
   372.2101–dc22
            2010036869

ISBN13: 978-0-415-57420-4 (hbk)
ISBN13: 978-0-415-57421-1 (pbk)
ISBN13: 978-0-203-82963-9 (ebk)

My thanks to the many friends who put up with hearing about my difficulties in writing this book as I struggled to condense the vast and varied and complex body of work produced over decades by the indefatigable Bruner into one slim and accessible volume. And thanks mostly to my friend Hazel Abel who read through the third draft for me and, as she has done by critically reading my books in the past, gave me the benefit of her perceptive and unique insights. Last but not least to my friend and fellow lover of literature in all its forms, the poet and storyteller, academic and thinker, Michael Rosen.

Contents

Acknowledgements

Extracts from *Carrying the Elephant: A Memoir of Love and Loss* by Michael Rosen (Harmondsworth: Penguin, 2002 pp. 1, 47) (© Michael Rosen, 2002) is printed by permission of Penguin Books Ltd and United Agents (www.unitedagents.co.uk) on behalf of Michael Rosen.

Introduction

This book is a companion volume to *Introducing Vygotsky* (Smidt, 2009) and has been written for all those who work with young children in some capacity to help them come to understand the thoughts and ideas of Jerome Bruner. Bruner's life covers much of the last century and the first decade of this and over that long period Bruner has seen many changes in thinking and emphasis and has contributed to debates not only about psychology but also about education, anthropology, biology, linguistics and other disciplines.

In the companion volume about Vygotsky there was a glossary of terms at the end of each chapter. In this book the complete glossary of Bruner's terms occurs at the end of the book. Some of these terms may be unfamiliar to you so you are invited you to use the glossary in order to look up new and unfamiliar terms you encounater as you read.

The book proper then starts with something about his life and about the main themes Bruner addressed in his writing and gives an idea of some of the many, many people who influenced him. The chapters that follow are devoted to exploring these themes, particularly in terms of how they relate to young children, their care and education. At the end of each of these chapters there is a section focusing on the implications for practice. As in the Vygotsky book the chapters all end with looking back and looking ahead. In this way what has been said is briefly summarised and an indication is given of what is to come next.

Chapter 1

The early life and times of Jerome Bruner

Introduction

In this opening chapter we look at what we know about the life and times of Bruner. We know a great deal, partly because he is still alive – aged ninety-four – and partly because he has written so much, including a book of auto-biographical essays. In a long and full and complex life he has influenced the thinking of many people, and his work has focused on aspects of perception, cognition and constructivism, the links between anthropology and psychology, mind, learning, language, culture, literature and curriculum. Although he spent most of his life working in his home country, he enjoyed nine years as Watts Professor of Psychology and Fellow of Wolfson College at Oxford University in the UK. It was here that his interest in cognitive development in infancy flourished and here that his reputation as a fighter for improved early childhood education developed.

Beginnings

Jerome Bruner was born in 1915 and grew up in a well-to-do middle-class family in New York. His parents, Herman and Rose, were Polish immigrants, and Jerome was the youngest of four. He was born blind, and it required two cataract operations when he was two years old to allow him to see. Yet he himself states in his wonderful autobiographical book *In Search of Mind* (Bruner 1983a) that his initial blindness had not 'crippled' him in any way, although he recognised that it may certainly have shaped him in some way. He says that the lack of peripheral vision which was the effect of the cataract operations made him continually have to move his head to see properly, and this, he says, 'gave me a specious air of great alertness' (Bruner 1983a: 14), and he relates this to the James-Lange theory which states that if we are sad because we cry then perhaps he, Bruner, was more alert because he had to move his head to keep up with life around him. This is our first encounter with Bruner's sense of humour.

After his sight had been restored, the family lived in what was then a somewhat remote suburb of New York: Far Rockaway. They lived in a substantial comfortable house with a field of meadow grass behind it. It was a large and extended family. Apart from his parents there was Uncle Simon and Aunt Sarah. Then, in descending order of age, came his older sister Min, his half-brother Adolf and two cousins, all roughly ten or fifteen years older than Jerome. Then came Jerome himself, his sister Alice (two years older) and two more cousins, Marvin and Julia. Alice, born when Min was already fourteen, was 'a mistake', says Bruner, but he was 'conceived out of my mother's conviction that it is better to raise children in pairs', and he jokes that he was 'the child of a theory' (Bruner 1983a: 10).

It was a traditionally Jewish family, and Bruner says that being a Jew has been a constant, if a sometimes problematic feature of his life, as constant a feature as being regarded as being 'bright' (Bruner 1983a: 7). The neighbourhood was a mixed one, and the family attended the local orthodox synagogue, but his father left that after a while and moved on to join the reform movement and a more modern synagogue.

Bruner's description of his parents is unsentimental. He saw his father as rather a remote figure, someone who travelled for business and who was often absent from the family. To Bruner he seemed a somewhat adventurous figure. But he was a good storyteller (and this is significant as you will see as you read on) and a man of strong principles. Bruner illustrates this with the story of how, on one occasion, when he had been sent to buy a newspaper for his father he brought home a copy of Hearst's paper *Journal*. His father was furious and scolded the child, telling him that Hearst was a wicked man who would do anything, even start a war, to sell his paper. For Bruner this was not a scolding but a tutorial. Bruner's father was a reader, a music lover, a conversationalist, a conservative in politics, a snob and a social climber. He had a taste for lovely things. So he was a complex man, and his youngest son followed in his footsteps in many ways.

His mother was a woman who displayed little joyfulness or playfulness in her relationships with her children. When it emerges that she had fled from a ghetto in Poland where she had witnessed people fleeing and houses set on fire it is easy to understand her apparent lack of joyfulness. But for the young Jerome this lack of joyfulness marked his early years. It was she who first made him aware of what it meant, at that time, to be Jewish. He says that she never told him a story other than that of her early traumatic experiences in Poland. He shared nothing with her or she with him, and she showed little affection to her children. She also avoided ever praising them. He believed that this was linked to a sense of not wanting her children to become arrogant or to believe that they were special. Her own life experiences had shown her the dangers of this.

When Bruner was about six years old, the family moved to a new neighbourhood, and he went to school and started to make friendships away from the earlier ones with siblings and cousins. He was able to walk to school with his friends, and his views on his early education are interesting and certainly contribute to the passions he developed when he became a psychologist, a researcher and a writer. For him, school was dull and puzzling. He was eager to please and tried hard to do what he was told to do but was not always successful because he was never quite clear about what he had been asked to do. It is interesting that this man who has influenced the education of generations of children showed no evident intellectual curiosity. His family took little interest in school, and there was nothing in his early academic record that revealed the promise of an academic career. The only intellectual experience he remembered was what he calls his encounter with light years, through his reading of *The Book of Knowledge*, a children's encyclopaedia. He found out that some stars were many million light years away – so far that they would travel for millions of years after they were extinguished. He found this such an astounding thought that it brought tears to his eyes as he looked at the night sky. He was eleven years old.

There was one teacher in his early schooling who impressed him. Her name was Miss Orcutt, and she talked to him of magical things such as molecules and Brownian motion. It was at this time that his father fell ill. Bruner, as a child, pleased to have his father at home more often, did not know that his father was dying of cancer. In the last months of his father's life, Bruner had two nightmares. They are worth recording for what they tell us about the trauma of this early loss. They also illustrate how this young boy perceived many things in terms of problems to be solved. In the first nightmare, the young Jerome dreamed that everybody in the world had died. He was the sole survivor until a new generation appeared. The dilemma posed in the dream was how he could possibly tell them everything that had been known before. Perhaps this explains why to this day Bruner still has his father's bound copy of the encyclopaedia, *The Book of Knowledge*. In the second dream Bruner is in a wasteland where there are no tracks. He is in some sort of wheeled vehicle. The problem he must solve is choosing a direction in which to go. This, says Bruner, was a choice that was 'appalling and would wake me terrified' (Bruner 1983a: 16).

In what he calls the last year of childhood he faced severe and tragic losses in his life, in addition to the loss of his father. His sister Min got married and left the home, and there was a fierce family dispute which caused Bruner to lose touch with his beloved cousins. In the months that followed he had two more disturbing dreams. In the first, an egg in a plain white egg cup cracks as he looks at it, and he is filled with terror. In the other he holds the secret knowledge of where he has hidden his father's body.

Through his ambivalent relationship with his father, which he analysed later in life when he became a psychologist, Bruner took on a set of values as an adolescent communist and what he called a premature anti-fascist, denouncing the world of money and business although pragmatically never refusing the benefits bestowed on him by the trust fund his father had left to see him through college.

Adolescence

After the death of his father Bruner's life became marked by movement and transition. He noted that his mother seemed to have come to life after the loss of her husband. Startlingly, her clothing became more colourful and bright. But she could not settle anywhere, and the effect of this was that Bruner attended six different high schools in four years. He discovered the pleasures of living close to the water. He explored canals and the harbour, took up fishing and acquired a boat with an outboard motor. Despite what he calls his 'appalling secondary schooling', his scholastic record was good, and he attempted many things, including running. But he felt it was a period of becoming self-conscious and ashamed of being Jewish. He talks of being a loner, someone who did not fit into any of the categories. He began to read widely: novels, travel books and poetry. He began to meet girls. In 1933 he went to college, to become a freshman at Duke University. He was seventeen, and Hitler had just come to power. Roosevelt had been elected. The country was deep into the Depression. Bruner's life was about to change.

In the chapter in his autobiography describing his transition to adulthood he writes about the role of play in childhood. He was thinking about how the kind of commitment and the depth of commitment come about through socialisation within a community as young people and children begin modelling themselves on others or on the roles that are defined by their group. It is worth quoting here exactly what he says:

> I suppose one of the distinctive things about play in childhood is that it buffers the player against too literal a commitment to whatever it is one is playing at, while at the same time giving the player a chance to explore possibilities. Many societies, indeed, are said to be highly permissive about play (and commitment?) in childhood and then mark by strict ceremony the 'passing out' into adulthood, at which point the child becomes a man or woman with strict limitations on what remains possible.
>
> (Bruner 1983a: 20)

Bruner felt that there was little within his family that led him to seek deep commitment to anything. When he emerged from childhood he felt that he had become part of a world he did not understand. His father was dead; his family were scattered; his schooling had been disrupted; and it appeared to him that going to college offered him his first home after childhood. It was there, in this 'home', that he began to feel deeply and learned to commit himself politically, intellectually and academically.

Becoming a freshman at college

Bruner became a freshman at Duke and said that his first months were social, tribal, perfect – he calls this 'an easy entry to the anteroom of grown-up society' (1983a: 22). After that semester, however, things started to change, and for the first time in his life he encountered anti-Semitism when he was refused entry to a particular fraternity that did not accept Jews. At this time he drifted into a set which he described as being 'brainy'. He developed a sense of identity and community and his choice for further study was psychology. After completing his undergraduate studies he moved on to graduate work. The times – the late 1930s – created something of a pressure-cooker atmosphere with intense political and intellectual discussion taking place everywhere. It was the time of the New Deal, the Japanese invasion of Manchuria, Mussolini's attack on Ethiopia. Hitler was lurking in the wings and the restlessness created by these significant and frightening events on the world stage was evident even in the smug and isolated atmosphere of Duke.

Bruner began to be aware of his own ideas and to become something of a rebel. He refused to attend chapel (a college requirement), wrote to the college paper and was labelled as a troublemaker. It was a label he liked, and he remains delighted that it sometimes applies to him to this day. Academically, within his chosen discipline of psychology, things were also polarised and politicised. The debate was about 'whether learning was passive, incremental and a mirror, or whether it was stepwise, discontinuous and driven by hypothesis' (Bruner 1983a: 27). In other words, was learning just taking in knowledge primarily through imitation or was it an uneven process involving the learner actively asking questions and seeking to find answers. Those who were opposed to the first, the continuity view, said it made man appear just a creature of his environment. They proposed the opposite view, that learning was driven by internally generated hypotheses either confirmed or refuted by events. We will return to this throughout the book. It was at this time that Bruner was introduced to the work of anthropologists, through the work of his friend Leonard Broom. This was to be one of the most important threads in his academic life.

His last year at Duke was 1938, marked by the bitter winding down of the Spanish Civil War. Bruner was invited to become a member of a Marxist study group, which he did, and he even played at being part of a communist cell for a while. After much thought and consideration, he moved on to Harvard.

Moving on to Harvard

Bruner spent the summer before starting at Harvard reading so when he arrived he was 'full of psychology' (Bruner 1983a: 32) although not quite knowing what to expect of his future studies in the field. In Harvard, at that time, the dominant strand within the psychology faculty was that of psychophysics, which involved a study of the senses and how they respond to external physical energies or stimuli. Bruner revolted against this and later, together with Leo Postman, set out on a series of experiments that resulted in what became known as the 'New Look', a revolutionary theory of perception. This held that perception is not something that occurs immediately but is a way of processing information involving selection and integration. This is a view of psychology that emphasises how people go beyond responding to stimuli to viewing and interpreting the world. It takes a more constructivist approach to perception and learning, seeing the learner as active and not passive. It is important in the analysis of his work, as will emerge throughout the book.

His time at Harvard was productive: he found the teaching style of the master–student relationship (an academic apprenticeship, perhaps) pleasing, and he became involved with fellow students, some of whom became lifelong friends. Bruner found that experimental psychology was where his interests lay, and he greatly enjoyed the topics covered – many of which became dominant themes of his own thinking and research, such as memory, perception, learning, motivation, neuro-psychology and animal behaviour. He greatly enjoyed the seminars where each of the graduate students presented a topic which was then followed by a free-for-all discussion. You can see how his awareness of not only what he was learning but also about how he was learning became an essential strand of his thinking.

All this took place to the backdrop of events in far-off Europe. Bruner described himself as being both a leftist and an interventionist in his feelings, wanting America to throw its weight behind Europe and to emerge from isolation. He developed a visceral and lifelong hatred of Hitler. By the time he got to the stage of writing his thesis he was so involved in the war that he chose as his topic the nature of the propaganda broadcasting of belligerent nations. He had visited Europe in the summer of 1939 as it veered towards war and had also met and married his first wife, Katherine.

The war years

Bruner worked initially at the Foreign Broadcast Monitoring Service in Washington, and his job was to monitor 'enemy' broadcasts although the USA was not yet at war. Later he was offered and accepted a job at Princeton, as Associate Director of the Office of Public Opinion Research, and he moved there with his wife and young son Whitley. It was during this phase that he first met Robert Oppenheimer and was fascinated by his brilliant mind, although he did not know in what work Oppenheimer was engaged at that time. But the bond of a love of psychology and the philosophy of physics was the basis for a firm and lasting friendship. Bruner grew restive and wanted to be more directly involved in what was happening in Europe and moved first to London and then to France, working for the Office of War Information. Still later his project became what was called 'cultural relations with the French university world', and whilst he was engaged in this he was in the privileged position of meeting and forming friendships with some of the great thinkers of the time. One of these was Sartre, who dominated the post-war Parisian cultural and intellectual scene. Eventually, despite the glamorous setting of Paris and the access to famous thinkers and artists, he began to miss university life and returned to Cambridge, Massachusetts, where he remained for the next twenty-seven years. It was here that his daughter was born and where his children grew up, went to school and eventually left to live independent lives. His son Whitley went on to be what Bruner calls an 'Arabist diplomat' and his daughter Jane a photographer.

Looking back, looking ahead

In this opening chapter we have looked at aspects of Bruner's childhood and his early life, up till the end of the Second World War. We have learnt something about his early childhood, the possible effects of his early blindness and the loss of his father, and the impact of the war in Europe into which America was eventually drawn. In the next chapter we turn our attention to his work post-war, paying particular attention to the people whom he met who influenced his thinking. We are moving from the young student to the mature man.

Chapter 2

The life of the mind of Jerome Bruner

Introduction

In this second chapter we turn our attention to a brief outline of the main themes of Bruner's professional life and to those who influenced him on the way. This is a scene-setting chapter and offers the reader an idea of some of the things we will be going into in more detail in the chapters that follow. The chapter draws on Bruner's autobiographical essays *In Search of Mind* where the title itself tells us that he wanted to write more than a simple autobiography: rather, he had decided to write the history of the development of his own mind. He set the scene like this:

> There is a way that things are different when one gets to the life of mind. You discover as an 'intellectual' that you have walked on stage into a drama already well scripted by others, a drama that has been going on for centuries before you made your entry. Your own intentions and thoughts become linked to ideas, issues and institutions that have long had a reality of their own. Karl Popper calls this world where ideas and paradigms and truths live independently of their origins World Three, a world of 'objective knowledge'.
>
> (Bruner 1983a: 56)

It is obvious that we are all influenced by others in our thinking, our learning and our work. Bruner charted some of the people who influenced him in the early years of being a psychologist as he worked on perception and learning and in his later work. We have already seen how he was influenced by the people he met through the war years from people as disparate as philosophers, artists, writers and statesmen.

Perception and the development of mind

Perception is a word not often used nowadays but at the time Bruner started his work as a psychologist many were involved in thinking about it. Bruner said that the world (and everything in it) is not just as you see it but it is as you see it in context and in relation to your thoughts. So things may look different depending on how you feel, who you are with, what you have just been doing, what you are thinking about and so on. Think about how differently you view the world when you open the curtains to a sunny day to how you view it on a dark and wet one.

There is a link between perception, mind and learning. Leo Postman was a colleague and friend with whom Bruner worked over a decade spanning the 1940s to 1950s. Together they shared ideas, wrote papers and collaborated on work on perception. One of the most famous of the Bruner–Postman studies was known as the 'red spade experiment'. They set about looking at an aspect of perception, that of people responding to what they see in terms of their expectations. In a pack of playing cards the spades are always black. Through experience of playing with cards you will expect the spades to always be black and the hearts always to be red. To examine how people deal with incongruities or anomalies in the world, Bruner and Postman decided to base their research on what seemed to be an ordinary pack of cards but in which the colours had been swapped over. The premise was that changing the colour of a suit would cause some concern to those looking at the cards. To measure the results they used a machine called a tachistoscope. A tachistoscope is a device that displays an image for a specific amount of time. This is usually done by projecting the image onto a screen. Tachistoscopes use a slide or transparency projector equipped with the mechanical shutter system typical of a camera. The slide is loaded, the shutter locked open and focusing and alignment are adjusted. Then the shutter is closed. When ready for the test, a shutter speed is selected, and the shutter is tripped normally.

The subjects were seated in front of a tachistoscope, and the subjects were shown both normal cards and anomalous cards, one at a time, each with a longer exposure time until the subject recognised and named them. The results were astounding. They showed that the viewers needed more time to identify the anomalous cards, not surprisingly, but once they had encountered a card with red spades on, for example, they hesitated more and took longer identifying the normal cards. It was as though seeing something that did not fit their expectation meant they had to adjust the expectation itself. For Bruner and Postman this meant that recognition involves more than just being able to identify what a thing is. It requires consideration of what a thing might be. For them it was the start of the whole area of what has come to be known as cognitive sciences.

Another person who influenced Bruner was Edward Tolman, who came to Cambridge from Berkley in 1951. It was his approach to learning theory that interested Bruner. As we have said, the prevailing view of learning was largely that of passive learners, dependent on repeated stimulation or input and on being rewarded for perceived successes. This relates to the work of Pavlov, who talked of 'conditioned reflexes' to explain learning. Through experimentation on animals Pavlov had concluded that when an animal that had previously salivated in the presence of food began to salivate when a buzzer associated with food was sounded, this learned or conditioned reflex (salivation to the buzzer) replaced the simpler reflex of salivating in the presence of food. For Tolman, however, learning was more complex than this: it involved a change in one's knowledge of the environment, and this was represented by what he called an internal and retained cognitive map. Working with rats and mazes but operating with a more cognitive and purposive approach allowed him to compare learning to the construction of a cognitive map. So for him learning was not a simple stimulus–response act but something that involved the learner in actively constructing some sort of mental map.

It was after a symposium in Boulder Colorado in 1955, after he had listened to the papers of both Heider and Festinger, and then presented his own seminal paper 'Going Beyond the Information Given', that he began to move on to thinking about man as a rational being, a thinker, a problem-solver, with a capacity for discrimination and the ability to select, classify, arrange and order. This is, in essence, the discipline of cognitive science.

Meaning and culture

For Bruner, meaning has always been at the heart of any investigation into mind and cognition. When we talk of meaning we are talking about making sense of something, of understanding or comprehending it. What made Bruner unusual and special in terms of Western psychologists at the time was his recognition that meaning is not determined by the biological needs we inherit, nor is it determined by individual thought: rather, it comes about through an active search for meaning within the context of a culture. This is a very important point so we will pause here in order to define both context and culture.

- Context, in the sense in which it is used here, means where something takes place where the word 'where' does not refer only to place but more widely to include with whom, in what circumstances, in what way and so on.
- Culture, in the sense in which it is used here, means all the ways groups have worked out of passing on the things that matter to them: the behaviour patterns, norms, language, the arts and crafts, the rituals and beliefs and values and principles and structures and institutions.

We make meaning as we seek to understand, interpret and explain the world and the objects and people in it. Each of us lives in one world but within that one world are many cultures, and we live primarily in one culture. As we try to make sense of the world we are trying to make sense of our own cultural world, and we use the things our culture has created (cultural tools) to help us make sense of the world.

All of this led Bruner to make links with other disciplines – significantly with anthropology but also with other interpretive social sciences. Interpretive social sciences are those that seek to understand and explain what is seen and heard. They go beyond mere description. One of the key influences which led him to become so interdisciplinary in his thinking was his earlier association with his roommate, the young anthropologist Leonard Broom. Broom, at the time, was interested in and critical of the work of Freud, and Bruner, too, became interested in some aspects of the work of Freud. Much later in his life he began to be interested in Freud's thinking about childhood as a tragic and family drama being responsible for the development of personality. By and large, though, he was critical of Freud.

It was the work of both Piaget and Vygotsky that led Bruner to broaden his interest in the mind and to see the vital role of culture and context in this development. Piaget's approach had been to focus on the development of logic – the ways in which a child attempted to solve a problem or to explain something. Bruner agreed with some aspects of Piaget's work, disagreed with much of it, but felt that overall Piaget had to be reckoned as one of the great pioneers. It was the work of Vygotsky that spoke more to him when he first encountered this in the late 1940s. He thought of Vygotsky as brilliant, passionate and utterly compelling, particularly with his insistence that the role of context and culture in the development of mind could not be ignored.

The Oxford years

By 1966, Bruner's interests began to move on to looking at early infancy in order to understand more about the development of mind. He drew on the work of Noam Chomsky, whose work first became known in the late 1950s. Chomsky criticised the mechanistic view of language acquisition and learning presented by Skinner and went on to consider the possibility of infants being born with the capacity to process language. For Bruner, what was fascinating in Chomsky's work of the time was his view that language is processed not through past experience but through the active nature of mind and brain. It was the beginning of perceiving of the human infant as being competent.

It was in 1970 that Bruner was invited to go to Oxford. For him this represented a dream opportunity: to live and work at a university so famous that its very name called up images of study and serious scholarship. In Bruner's words, 'it is tautly serious ... judgmental, hierarchical and unforgiving. It marks you ... Purity and intellectual impeccability, those are the ideals' (Bruner 1983a: 253, 255). It was here that his work took on an additional dimension and one that is of particular interest to those working and concerned with young children. He became interested in the learning of infants and young children, particularly in how they acquired and used language.

Bruner gathered a research group around him, and this group included some brilliant and innovative researchers and thinkers, some of whom have become almost household names. Amongst them was Hanus Papousek, who had fled Czechoslovakia and joined Bruner's research group in Oxford. He worked extensively on mother–infant interactions. Also working in the group was Colwyn Trevarthen, who was working on aspects of perception, focusing on detail and context. Then there was Berry Brazelton, who was working on the early development of mother–infant interaction, focusing on the differences between that and infants' reactions to inanimate objects, and Roger Brown, who was working on what he called 'first language', which meant the small number of meanings that early speech was about. It will be clear to you that the focus of this Oxford research group was the transition from prelinguistic to linguistic competence.

Around this time, Chomsky's LAD (Language Acquisition Device) fell into disfavour, mainly because it paid scant attention to prior learning and to the need to communicate with others. In other words, it largely ignored the social. Some saw it as being too mechanistic, and for Bruner it was clear that more attention needed to be paid to the purposes and uses for language. It was in response to this that he developed the Language Acquisition Support System (LASS).

Pedagogy, education and curriculum

Always a deeply political man with a concern for the well-being of others, Bruner became concerned at what he observed to be happening to children as they entered formal education in schools. In the USA after the war, along with the rapid development of the teaching of mathematics and science in schools, the perceived and the real failure of groups of children began to be apparent. The groups were mainly poor and mainly black. As Bruner put it, poverty was 'discovered'. The outcome of this was an attempt to 'compensate' for what was perceived to be missing from the lives of poor children, and the Head Start programmes began. Bruner started travelling in Africa and thinking more deeply about the importance of culture and the ways in which it affected how children behaved in learning situations. Around this time he met Luria, one of Vygotsky's colleagues, who was convinced of the vital roles of language and culture in the functioning of mind. Bruner summarised his thoughts in his 1996 book *The Culture of Education*. The basic underpinning argument of the book is that the mind only reaches its full potential through participation in the culture and that this involves more than sciences and arts in the most formal sense to include perceiving, thinking, feeling and carrying out discourse. In the book he also talks of the spiral curriculum, which is something we will return to later in the book.

Narrative: making stories

Later in his life, Bruner began to focus on the role of narrative (or the making of stories) in mediating human experience and action. He saw narrative as a way of reasoning, as a form of language and as a cultural tool (and here he draws on Vygotsky) for making sense in an ongoing way, for structuring action and for building a self-identity. Some writers say that he is developing a narrative view of culture and mind in which he argues that reality is narratively constructed. His arguments are complicated, and we will deal with them in more detail later in the book. The influences on his thinking here come primarily from anthropology and the seminal work of Claude Lévi-Strauss and Clifford Geertz.

Looking back, looking ahead

In this chapter we have started to examine some of the main themes in Bruner's work through looking at some of the people he encountered or worked with and who had some influence on his thinking, at his research and at his writing. You will recognise that this is very much just a 'taster' of some complex ideas which will be developed in the chapters that follow. We now start to look at these ideas in more detail and will begin with Bruner's ideas on mind and meaning.

Chapter 3

Mind and meaning

Introduction

This is the first chapter devoted to an in-depth examination of some of Bruner's key thoughts. We start by looking at what he wrote about how children come to be able to understand their world and the objects and people in it. Bruner called this the development of mind. We might also call it the development of cognition or thinking. His early work here is important to understanding how his thinking developed over time so we continue to pay attention here to those whose work had some influence on his thinking. Writing in the 1960s, Bruner began his consideration of how mind or intelligence develops by looking at two crucial things that set humans apart from other mammals. He looked at the development and the importance of tools.

Standing on two legs: becoming a tool user

In his occasional paper *'The Growth of Mind'* (1966b), Bruner stated that what set humans apart was initially the ability to stand upright, releasing the upper limbs for other purposes – particularly for fashioning and using tools. It was the use of tools that was most significant in the development of cognition: that and the development of language. Bruner pointed out that physiologically humans had evolved to have a large brain, a small jaw and less ferocious teeth than other creatures. The niche that humans eventually filled, after forming groups with others, was born out of these features. At first the making of tools dominated, but it seems that human beings were almost pre-programmed to fit the tools they made into sequences of action. Let us examine how this might happen.

- In order to make a mark, man developed and used a sharp tool – perhaps a pebble. He was then able to make a mark on a flat surface.
- If he wanted to vary the colour of the mark he might use a burned twig or mix mud with water.

- If he needed to hunt and kill creatures he developed a bow and arrow, a line with a hook on the end of it, a net and so on.

Once human beings had lived in settled groups for some time, the tools they made became more complex, and when new tools were needed individuals used the templates of existing tools to make these. In order to use new tools, existing skills might need to be extended. So human beings not only needed to make tools but also needed to develop and refine the skills required to use them effectively. Those living in settled groups shared their tools and their practices: they shared a culture and began to pass on their tools and skills and knowledge from one generation to the next. This was the birth of cultural transmission.

Another feature of human development noted by Bruner is that the human infant, at birth, is immature both physically and in terms of cerebral development. It takes considerably longer for the human infant to achieve physical maturity than any other species, and this allows for a prolonged time for the necessary skills to be transmitted.

Different cultures, different tools, different skills

We turn now to examining some of Bruner's ideas and research that cause some people to feel anxious. This is because it seems that he is talking about 'civilisation' and that he sees some societies as less developed or civilised than others. His findings are interesting and worth reading, and you are, of course, free to reject anything that disturbs you. It is important to say that he, himself, was aware of the sensitivities relating to this work. In his desire to track the evolution that took place between what he calls 'hominids' (or baboons) and humans he used film of the infants of hunter-gatherer peoples living in the Kalahari desert in Africa. The !Kung are part of the San group of peoples, and, although they were clearly without technology or a written language, they lived in social groups, used language, developed and used tools and engaged in rituals.

When studying the development of mind, Bruner noted that the baboons living in social groups within a territory displayed different gender roles. It was the adult male baboons who demonstrated what might be called the expected dominance/protective patterns and protected the female and young by engaging in joint action against predators. What Bruner focused on was the behaviour of young baboons who seemed to show signs of practising male and female roles in their play with one another. It appeared that play offered opportunities for both spontaneous expression and those colla-borative actions that in adulthood became the behaviour of the dominant male or the infant-protective female. No evidence of the participation of any adult baboons in this play was evident. Nor do baboons ever seem to play with objects or imitate directly sequences of adult baboon behaviour.

So, Bruner suggests, the baboons used play as preparation for adult roles. For him there was little evidence of this play being linked to the development of mind or cognition/thinking.

He then examined the behaviour of the infants in the hunter-gatherer groups. They, by contrast, were in a community where constant interaction between adult and child or adult and adolescent or adolescent and child was evident. They played and sang and danced together, sat together to eat, went on minor hunting trips together, enjoyed song and storytelling together. Often the children were spectators at or participants in ritual events – such as the first haircut or the first killing of a buck or, for boys, the process of scarification, the ritual cutting denoting rite of passage from childhood to adulthood. The children play and their play is imitative in that they use the rituals, the implements, the tools, the weapons and the language of their adult world. It is clear that they are learning through observation, imitation, participation and interaction even though in the films there is not one single episode of any teaching using telling. Where there is anything we might call instruction, this takes place through showing, or modelling. Children are not seen to practise or repeat anything except through play where they use play itself to adopt and try out adult roles and feelings. So there are examples of children playing at hunting or bossing or looking after baby or making and keeping house. Bruner said, 'In the end, every man in the cultures knows nearly all there is to know about how to get on with life as a man, and every woman as a woman – the skills, the rituals and myths, the obligations and rights' (Bruner 1966b: 6).

Bruner then turned his attention to more complex societies where he found obvious changes in the instruction of young children. He said that this is due partly to the fact that in such societies there is vastly more knowledge and skill than that held by one individual or one group. In order to simplify the passing on of skill and knowledge, the more economical technique of telling out of context rather than showing in context developed. You will have realised that the ways in which children were instructed in the San community was by being shown how to do things in context. In literate societies, such as ours, what has happened is that the practice of telling out of context has become institutionalised in the school and the teacher. And both the school and the teacher promote this necessarily abstract way of instructing the young. So a body of knowledge is put together according to what some regard are the needs of the young at different ages and stages, and this becomes the curriculum – what is to be taught and learned. In some countries the curriculum is centrally determined. In other countries the curriculum may be regionally determined, as in areas of Italy. It takes little thought to recognise that often what is taught has little to do with life as it is lived by those in the society. The school then is very far from local or indigenous practice. This becomes even more marked in places where there are peoples from different cultures living together. Learning is expected to take place out of context in terms of the lives, experiences and interests of the children, and this may well be why, for so many pupils, school seems irrelevant. You may remember that Bruner himself felt that schooling was irrelevant, despite the fact that he recognised that schooling per se was a very significant thing in the lives of most people and that the existence of schools may free learners from a very narrow or local way of thinking and offer them other possible worlds. The school could and should be the ideal place to encourage children to think, to reflect on things, to ask questions and to set about solving them. The school may also assist in the development of the use of highly abstract uses of symbolic forms and language – both spoken and written. Through this children become able to think about the past, about the future and about real and possible worlds.

Bruner goes on to talk of what he calls *amplification systems*, and what he means by this are the tools, physical and cognitive, which are used by human beings to assist them in making and sharing meaning. He is talking of what Vygotsky called cultural tools and explains amplification systems like this. Amplification systems include the following:

- tools to enhance action: things like hammers, levers, sticks, wheels and spades;
- tools to enhance or amplify the senses: things like smoke signals, microphones, magnifying glasses, telescopes, diagrams;
- tools to amplify thought: things like symbolic systems (alphabets and scripts, books and numbers), computers, electronic devices, logic and so on.

In Bruner's words, a culture then is 'a deviser, a repository and a transmitter of amplification systems and of the devices that fit into such systems' (1966b: 7). In other words, each culture develops its own tools, uses, keeps and shares them and deploys them to pass on the knowledge, customs, skills, values, beliefs, rituals and practices developed within the culture. The tools developed, held and used within a hunter-gatherer community will be more practical and related to action than those in a more complex society, where the tools are more symbolic, more abstract and more verbal.

Cultural transmission: equipping the young

Bruner wrote about what he believed any society needed to do in order to equip its young as learners. Clearly any society needs to gather together a body of knowledge and skills related to its culture and to convert them into a suitable format for beginner learners. In other words, a society needs to agree a curriculum or syllabus to be put in place for formal learning and also to ensure that it is presented in a way that will match the ages, needs, styles of learning and experience of the learners. Those of us in England are familiar with the ongoing debates about what very young children need to learn. Do they need to learn phonics or should they be read to and invited to share books and only meet phonics once they have had such an introduction to books and reading? Do they need to learn how to write 'correctly' using traditional spelling or should they be allowed to experiment with writing, using their own ideas and hypotheses about how writing works? Should they have to sit down at tables or should they be free to move around and select to follow their own interests? Bruner suggested that learners need to be protected from what he called 'needless learning' and added that it was this that leads to children being grouped or taught or thought of according to ability. More questions arise from this. Should we have children in ability groups, thinly disguised by giving them the names of colours or shapes or animals or countries? What messages do children get from being in the top group? Or in the bottom group? Should we teach them in mixed-ability groups? If you have read the work of Lilian Katz you will know that she talks about children not being asked to do trivial things that are remote from both their experience and interests – things like making collages out of dried leaves or colouring in or doing worksheets.

Here we begin here to encounter two of the problems which seem to be endemic in schooling in developed or industrialised or complex societies. The first is that in our schools much of the teaching involves telling and much of the learning involves sitting down, listening and being passive. There is a separation of knowledge and action. And this, we suggest, is largely responsible for the fact that in developed countries the learning may be experienced by the children as irrelevant to their lives, their experience and context. You will remember that this is how Bruner himself recorded his own responses to his schooling.

Here are two vignettes. Read them through and think about how each of the children involved might be experiencing schooling.

- Three-year-old Shasti has just arrived in London from a village in Pakistan. On her second day, the teacher asks her to copy her name (written in English) from a card onto a piece of paper. Shasti does not yet understand English. Nor does she know what the marks on the card are or what she is being asked to do. Seeing her confusion, the teacher asks another older child to explain to Shasti in Urdu.
- Seven-year-old Honey has been reading one of the *Philip Pullman* books with her mother every evening. The book she has to read in class is a reading-scheme book which does not have a story that engages her interest.

You will realise that in the extreme case of Shasti the task is totally inappropriate to her previous experience and life. For her this is a bewildering experience taking place so early in her schooling career. It is fortunate that the newly qualified young teacher notices the child's bewilderment and takes steps to redress it. It is possible that the teacher in this case is too busy to have had time to consider the importance of allowing young learners to draw on their previous experience. In the case of Honey, the teacher, this time a mature and experienced teacher, also pays scant attention to her pupil's experience. Honey clearly is very fortunate in terms of the encounters she is having out of school with books and writers. There is no reason why the teacher should not take account of this and allow for it in her classroom.

For the hunter-gatherer children described earlier in this chapter, learning was clearly embedded within the context of life and action. Bruner insists that a society must ensure that the skills and procedures should remain intact from generation to generation. In many developed societies this is so, but sometimes – as in the case of black South Africans during the apartheid years, of the Incas and the Aztecs and Mayas and Easter Islanders – much of the culture was irretrievably lost through imperialism and colonialism. Here is a case study showing the impact of the loss of language and culture.

The Jotï are an indigenous group numbering about 800 individuals among 25 communities located in the Upper Cuchivero watershed in Bolívar State, and the Asita, Iguana, and Upper Parucito River basins in Amazonas State. The local environment is mainly tropical forest that varies in terms of structure and composition along an altitudinal gradient from basimontane to premontane to montane levels. The Jotï were totally isolated and uncontacted by the western world until the 1970's due to the difficult access and rugged mountainous terrain of their home territory. At that time, they were very nomadic and subsisted mainly by hunting-gathering but also practiced an incipient form of shifting cultivation. In the last three decades, some of them have expanded their contacts with neighboring indigenous groups and foreign missionaries, acquired western trade goods and tools, and been exposed to foreign cultural beliefs and practices. However, not all local groups are equally affected by these changes. Some groups continue to live a traditional nomadic lifestyle and have virtually no contact with nonJotï and even those who have settled around current or former mission bases still have very limited contact and interaction with outsiders and continue to depend heavily on foraging and trekking activities for their livelihood. As a result, the Jotï are rightly considered to be one of the least acculturated indigenous groups living in Venezuela today. Most members of their group are monolingual speakers of the Jotï language and relatively few people have learned Spanish as a second language.

(www.terralingua.org/projects/vitek/pilot.htm)

As a result of the documented experiences of many of the world's people (such as the one above) the United Nations Declaration on the Rights of Indigenous Peoples (2007) was drawn up and agreed. It seeks to redress the existing practices which denied many minority groups the rights to maintain their own culture. At least two of the articles are relevant to all those involved with the care and education of children.

Article 14 refers to the following:

- Indigenous peoples have the right to establish and control their educational systems and institutions, providing education in their own languages, in a manner appropriate to their cultural methods of teaching and learning.
- Indigenous individuals, particularly children, have the right to all levels and forms of education of the State without discrimination.
- States shall, in conjunction with indigenous peoples, take effective measures, in order for indigenous individuals, particularly children, including those living outside their communities, to have access, when possible, to an education in their own culture and provided in their own language.

Article 15 refers to the following:

- Indigenous peoples have the right to the dignity and diversity of their cultures, traditions, histories and aspirations which shall be appropriately reflected in education and public information.

The influence of Piaget and Vygotsky

We have already mentioned that, for Bruner, there were two theorists whose work had a tremendous significance. They were Jean Piaget and Lev Vygotsky, with views that were similar in some respects and radically different in others. Piaget's work is known throughout the world, and his influence continues to this day. For Bruner, his approach was dominated by epistemology and logic. Let us explore more closely the meanings of these terms.

- Epistemology is a branch of philosophy that studies the nature of knowledge, its presuppositions and foundations and its extent and validity. In essence it asks four questions: What is knowledge? How is it acquired? What do people know? and How do we know what we know?
- Logic is the science of correct reasoning, which describes relationships among propositions in terms of implication, contradiction, contrariety, conversion and so on. Logic is used in most intellectual activity but is concerned primarily in the disciplines of philosophy, mathematics, and computer science. Logic examines general forms which arguments may take, and considers which forms are valid, and which are fallacies. It is one kind of

critical thinking. In philosophy, the study of logic falls in the area of epis-temology, which asks (as we have said), 'How do we know what we know?'

Piaget set out to explain the underlying logic that allows knowledge to be constructed and passed on. He wanted to know how children were able to receive knowledge. He was famous for recognising that the learner was not a passive recipient of knowledge but an active constructor of it. In other words, he said that the child actively tries to make sense of the world and of the people in it. He was little concerned with the nature of the world of the child, and it follows from that that he paid little, if any, attention to context or culture. Within his logical framework he saw the child as devel-oping through clear age-related stages, using the processes of assimilation (the shaping of experience to fit into one's mental schemata) and accommoda-tion (the changing of one's schemata to fit experience) in order to achieve equilibrium. For Bruner, equilibrium was a somewhat unclear concept. Bruner described what he thought the world of Piaget's growing child was like.

> He is virtually alone in it, a world of objects that he must array in space, time and causal relationships. He begins his journey egocentrically and must impose properties on the world that will eventually be shared with others. But others give him little help. The social reciprocity of infant and mother plays a very small role in Piaget's account of development. And language gives neither hints nor even a means of unravelling the puzzles of the world to which language applies. Piaget's child has one overwhelming problem: to bring the inner representations of mind into equilibrium with the structures of experience. Piaget's children are little intellectuals, detached from the hurly-burly of the human condition.
>
> (Bruner 1983a: 138)

Bruner's relationship with Piaget was thus a complicated one, and he talked of it as something of a father–son relationship. He was filled with respect for Piaget and for his work but aspects of the work bothered him, particularly the passivity implied by the stage theory of development. For Bruner, learning was a process of personal and active discovery, and although it was clear to him that thinking and reasoning became more sophisticated over time, a clear age-stage theory was too crude. His answer to this was to posit an alternative approach. It grew out of his ongoing interest in representation and briefly stated that children progressively move through three stages of learning as follows:

1. An *enactive stage* where children begin to develop understanding through actively manipulating objects. The implication is that this is the stage or phase where children learn through play and should be encouraged to play.

2.   An *iconic stage* where children become able to make mental images of something and no longer need to have the physical object or thing or experience in front of them. Children here use memory to store experiences and can use the mental images stored to refer to in order to help them understand things.

3.   The final stage is the *symbolic stage*, and here children can use abstract ideas to represent the world. The ability to use symbols and symbolic systems allows them to evaluate and make judgments and to think critically.

Bruner initially believed that children needed to move through these stages successively in order to make connections and to generate their own understandings.

Below you will find a case study showing the same child, over time, operating in each of Bruner's stages. You decide if this would be helpful to you in your practice.

- When Freedom was three years old, the teacher at his centre recorded this: 'Freedom has a new baby at home and today at nursery he went and got one of the dolls, put it in a pram and wheeled it around the garden. He then brought it into the room, took it out of the pram and smashed it hard against the table. We just watched him and didn't say anything but we thought it was worth making a note of it since it seemed to reflect his confused emotions.' (His response is enactive, using his senses, movement and exploring his feelings.)

- Two years later, when he was in the reception class, Freedom did a series of drawings which were included in his profile. In the first drawing there is a human figure which he says is 'me'. Then there is second drawing consisting of four figures – one very tall, one smaller, one even smaller and one just a dot: 'My family'. (His response is iconic, using pictures and images, and again he is exploring his feelings.)

- At the end of Year 2 Freedom wrote this: 'When my little sister was born I felt really angree. I wanted to be the only speshal one but my mum kept telling me that she loved us both the same and now my sister is kwit nice and we play together. I love my famlee.' (His response here is symbolic, using written language to express ideas and feelings.)

Do you agree with Bruner that children need to move through these stages successively? What about the child who writes fluently and also enjoys acting out emotions and feelings and making images of them?

Vygotsky's world was a very different place. Vygotsky's child grows up achieving consciousness and voluntary control, learning to speak and finding out what this means, taking over the forms and tools of the culture (at first clumsily but with growing skill and refinement) and then using these appropriately. For Bruner, the decisive feature of this view of the world of the learner was precisely the insistence that learning was rooted in culture and context, which made this view so novel and exciting. Vygotsky believed that learning took place through interaction between a more and a less experienced learner and involved the use of cultural tools – things such as books, language (spoken or written) and symbolic systems, all developed within the culture. He believed that the more experienced other was able to help the child move beyond a perceived level of achievement to a potential level of achievement and called this notional gap the zone of proximal development. His model of learning is that of the transmission or passing on of knowledge. The implications of this are that each child or learner is able to use the assistance of others (children or adults) to enable her to organise her thought processes so that she can do something on her own. It marks the move from dependence on help to independence. This focus on the importance of a more experienced other in the learning process is fundamental to Vygotsky's thinking and very influential on Bruner's.

So, as we have seen, for Bruner the role of a more experienced other in the learning process was fundamental. He saw the job of the teacher or educator as ensuring that assistance – carefully matched to the learner's needs at the time – be given through his three stages (discussed earlier) by a process he called *scaffolding*. You might want to think about how many parents and carers seem to do this instinctively. Bruner used the analogy of the scaffolding that is put up whilst a building is being constructed or restored. The scaffold that the adult erects allows the child to take small supported steps in learning, and when the child is able to manage without help the scaffold is removed.

It sounds quite straightforward, but it is something that requires considerable sensitivity and skill. You might want to think about what it is that the adult or more experienced person has to do to successfully scaffold learning. The example below gives some pointers to what needs to be done for scaffolding to be successful. First you will read the notes about what happened. Then you will read an analysis of what the more experienced other – Marva – did to scaffold Zac's learning.

- Zac said he wanted to make a boat out of found materials. He spent a considerable amount of time picking up one thing, looking at it and then putting it down again. The teacher, Marva, watching him, let him carry on doing this for some time without intervening, but when she noticed that he seemed unable to make a decision she went over and said, 'Are you looking for something special? Something important? I know it is for your boat.'
- 'I need something that it won't matter if it gets wet,' said Zac.

- 'Ah,' said Marva. 'I understand. You want something that can go in water without getting so wet that it will sink.'
- Zac nodded and smiled. Then he picked up a cardboard box. 'This would be good to put things in, but if I put it in the water it is going to get too wet and soggy.'
- Marva agreed and then held up a plastic egg box. He shook his head. 'It's too small,' he explained.
- 'Ah, you want something bigger and waterproof. Wait here for a minute. I think there are some more containers in the cupboard.'
- She went over to the cupboard and brought back a box full of plastic food containers, shiny foil containers, plastic lids, empty cans and toilet-roll holders. Zac explored each object carefully and then selected a plastic food container and set about making his boat.

Read through the observation notes again and jot down your own ideas of what the teacher, Marva, did to support Zac's learning. Now read through this and see if you agree.

Can you see how Marva took time to understand what it was that Zac was doing? She needed to do this in order to ensure that her intervention would be useful to him. He was able to explain the problem clearly, and she was then able to offer him an alternative to his first choice of cardboard box, which he rejected because it was the wrong size. This offered her the opportunity to repeat his assessment of the object (too small) and to introduce the word 'waterproof' to broaden his choice of words. You will remember he had used the words 'wet' and 'soggy'. So she paid attention to what he was doing and saying and tried to match her words and actions to what she perceived as his needs. She then provided him with some resources which he could sift through to make his own choice. So she scaffolded his learning through language (helping him vocalise his problem and enhancing his vocabulary) and through offering him resources. Finally he was able to make his boat unaided because her intervention had allowed him to make the crucial choice of container without assistance.

Marva's actions were quite simple but they were totally dependent on her being able to work out what it was that the child was interested in and in identifying what, if any, assistance he needed.

The implications for practice

In this chapter we find three of Bruner's ideas which are potentially useful for our practice as educators. These are:

1. *His focus on interaction between the learner and a more experienced other, with the more experienced other helping the child to move from being dependent on help*

to being independent. The teacher scaffolds the learning, and this is something we need to ensure that we do. Scaffolding is a highly skilled act, requiring the more experienced other (you as teacher or practitioner) to know and do several things:

- to understand what it is that the child is interested in, trying to do or paying attention to;
- based on that, to intervene in a way which will help the child achieve independence in that task (and this can be done through commenting on what the child has already achieved);
- to help the child to reflect on what she has been doing, suggesting particular resources and so on.

2. *The importance of context and culture in learning.* For us this means that we need to ensure that the contexts we provide make sense to the child and allow the child to build on prior experience. Learning should be about something that matters to the child and relates in some way to the child's culture. When you are planning to set up an activity or to bring in resources, you need to stop and ask yourself the following questions: Will all the children be able to relate to this? Does it reflect the experience of all the children? Is my choice of resources biased in any way? Am I using language that excludes some children? These are tough questions but ones you need to routinely ask.

3. *Bruner's representational stages – enactive, iconic and symbolic – may be useful to you if only in the sense that you pay attention to what children are using when they represent their thoughts and ideas.* You may notice that the child is relying primarily on movements and sensory exploration, on using pictures and images or on using symbolic systems. You may want to introduce alternative forms of representation if you feel that a child is stuck at one phase. For example, if the child does not want to use symbols you might want to ensure that the child has more concrete experience, building confidence. Or if the child is being pressured to do formal things (such as sums), you may want to invite the child to represent things enactively or iconically.

Looking back, looking ahead

In this, the first of the chapters looking in more depth at Bruner's ideas, we have looked at how children make sense of the world and the people in it. We started off by looking at the development of the human species and what made it special – namely, the development and use of tools and of the skills involved in using them. This drew us to look at this within different cultures to understand the effect this had on passing on the culture. And whilst thinking of this we began to consider what is taught and how it is taught in different groups at different times. We touched on the influence of Piaget and Vygotsky and ended the chapter looking at Bruner's idea of scaffolding. In the next chapter we continue our examination of competent children as we look at brilliant babies.

Chapter 4

Brilliant babies

Introduction

Bruner turned his attention to looking at early infancy in 1966. It was part of his research into how mind begins, and in this chapter we examine his developing ideas and theories. Again we talk about the people with whom he worked and who influenced his thinking. And again we look for implications his thoughts have for our practice.

Learning about the newborn

When Bruner began his investigations into the behaviour of infants all he knew was what could be found in the standard reference books of the time, and these focused on things such as reflexes and sensory processes and, not surprisingly, paid little or no attention to cognition or the mind. Experiments at the time used machines to measure things such as heart rate or skin conduction or other physiological changes. Bruner had had two children of his own by this time but apart from finding them fascinating he recognised that he knew little or nothing about infancy per se. He then met Berry Brazelton, who was a paediatrician and was developing a neonatal assessment test. Because of the focus on experience and context and interaction embedded in his work, you can see why Bruner believed that Brazelton was just the man to 'educate' him about infant behaviour. He started going with Brazelton on Saturdays to the Boston Lying-in Hospital and asked him questions about infants which both later described as 'outrageous'.

Brazelton understood that while babies may not speak their first word for a year or more, they are born ready to communicate, equipped with a rich vocabulary of body movements, cries and visual responses. We can regard all of these as part of the complex language of infant behaviour. You will realise the significance of this the more you read of this book. In order to try and understand what the behaviour of babies allowed people to understand about their needs and feelings and even thoughts, Brazelton and his colleagues developed a sort of measurement scale which Brazelton called his Neonatal

Behaviour Assessment Scale. It was aimed at parents, researchers and health-care providers and was designed to enable them to be able to interpret the physiological signs given. It considered a wide range of behaviours and was regarded as being suitable for examining newborns and infants up to the age of about two months. By the end of the assessment, Brazelton felt that the researcher would have what could be called a 'behavioural portrait' of the baby's strengths, adaptive responses and possible vulnerabilities.

At the time of its publication, the only other tests available were those looking for abnormalities. The new scale offered something new, and, for Bruner, one of the most significant things about it was the assumption that *all infants are competent and capable at birth*. Brazelton recognised that new-borns had already had nine months of experience *in utero* prior to birth and were able to control their behaviour in response to their environment. He also highlighted the significance of the fact that human infants could com-municate through their actions, their sounds, their gestures and their expressions. They could also respond to the cues around them (think about how an adult smile elicits a baby smile) and could recognise the fact that their actions could result in responses (think about the baby crying in order to get fed). Another assumption underlying the scale is that *each infant is an individual, born into social groups and ready to both be shaped by and to play a part in shaping their environment and their care*. This is a constructivist and interactionist approach (Brazelton 1995).

Later Brazelton went to work at the Centre for Cognitive Studies with Bruner and the team he was building around himself. Included in this team was the young Scot, Tom Bower, who was also interested in both infancy and how mind begins. He and Bruner conducted experiments, some of which were rather bizarre. One involved designing an experimental room in which to test the babies. They did this because of the fact that the existing test rooms were too cluttered perceptually. The room they designed was meant to be stimulus-free. What they found was that babies, placed in a special chair (which became known as 'the Harvard chair'), would become so distressed by having nothing to look at that they would burst into tears. Bower returned to Edinburgh and continued his work into the development of understanding about objects and about their permanence. He was very interested in the development of this in blind babies and later (in 1979) published a book called *A Primer of Infant Development*.

Bruner worked, too, in collaboration with a young woman called Ilze Kalnins. They had noticed that when infants watched pictures they almost invariably turned away from them if they were made to appear blurred or out of focus. They decided to try and see if the infants could improve the quality of the image using the sucking reflex and a dummy (or pacifier) connected to a focusing mechanism. They carried out the study and found that the babies at the age of about six weeks could indeed speed up their sucking to clear up a blurred image. More than that they found that babies could refine their technique of sucking to combine it with looking in order to create the effects that satisfied them. For Bruner and Kalnins this was clear evidence of intelligent behaviour. Bruner began to consider the *infant as an early hypothesis-maker* and stated that it was only the tendency to tire easily or lose concentration that made infant behaviour sometimes appear to be random. In Bruner's words, the infant's behaviour is 'labile', by which he meant that the child becomes easily frustrated or bored, particularly in a situation where the infant has no control of what happens. We see here the beginning of the sense of *agency*.

Soon after this the research team broadened to include Colwyn Trevarthen, Hanus Papousek and others, and the work gathered pace and was regularly reviewed in the press. The message coming across was that infants were more competent, more active and more organised in their thinking and their behaviour than had been thought before.

This was significant and far-reaching work, and research in this field continues today. Gopnik et al. (1999) remind us of the experiment showing that if you stick your tongue out at a baby, the baby will stick his or her tongue out at you. This seems like imitation, but in order to check that it wasn't just a chance happening, one of the team, Meltzoff, videoed babies' faces and showed the video to someone who had no idea what had started any of the responses. It was clear that the babies were, indeed, imitating. The first infants Meltzoff studied were three weeks old. He then decided to see if this imitative response was innate. In other words, were human infants born with the desire and the ability to imitate others? He set up a lab next to the labour room and was able to test babies soon after birth: the youngest was forty-two minutes old. This is fascinating, but we need to ask why it matters and what it shows about brilliant babies.

We can start to answer these questions by thinking about what a newborn baby has to know in order to imitate what an adult human being does with his or her face. In order to make the movements required to stick out one's tongue in response to seeing someone else do this, the baby needs to get feedback about what moving the tongue feels like. More than that, the baby, pre-programmed as we believe to respond to human faces, must also be able to work out that they have a face which is like that of others, with a mouth in which there is a tongue which can be stuck out. It looks simple, but it is, in effect, a complex task.

There is considerable research evidence that infants pay close attention to faces, voices and other aspects of other humans: they smile at a disc shape with a facial configuration on it and listen to the female voice more closely than to the male voice. Trevarthen tells us that at two months they are able to distinguish between someone who is going to communicate with them from someone who is not. By the time they are seven or eight months old they are keyed into the facial expressions of adults. By nine months they start to engage in peek-a-boo and hide-and-seek games and in the rituals surrounding bath time, bedtime and feeding time. What is happening is that babies are beginning to share a *communicative framework* which is made of words and gestures and facial expressions and signals and body language. Bruner tells us that their means to an end or ways of getting their needs or desires met begin to include the actions of other people. So infants' main tool for achieving their goals is another person. Babies are social and sociable beings, and their learning comes about primarily through the interactions with others and their growing ability to understand the motives and feelings of others.

The concept of deprivation and compensatory action

Bruner's work into early infancy and mind was taking place in the 1960s, which was a decade of political change and action characterised in the USA by the development of both the civil-rights movement and the women's movement. These social revolutions were demanding change in the lives and conditions of both black people and of women and, by extension, of the children of these people. Black children were routinely failing in schools, and working women needed affordable childcare to allow them to work outside of the home. Bruner's research on the competent infant was suggesting that the early years were crucial in development, and this became a factor in some of the compensatory programmes that arose. The best known of these was the Head Start program, on which the UK's Sure Start programme is based, which was started as part of President Lyndon Johnson's *War on Poverty* and was inspired partly by Bruner's research and also by what was known as the *'Little School of 400'*.

The Little School of 400 was an educational project developed in Texas by Felix Tijerina and the League of United Latin American Citizens during the 1950s. Tijerina was a Houston entrepreneur and civic leader who felt he knew the difficulties that Spanish-language children encountered because he had learned English with great difficulty as a youngster and thought that many of his own early problems in life had resulted from this language 'deficiency'. He seems not to have ever considered what part the lack of recognition of his skills in Spanish played. Adopting the pedagogy of language training prevalent during the time, Tijerina set out to provide English instruction for thousands of Mexican-American children, so he set up the Little School. Its aim was to teach Spanish-speaking pre-school children a speaking vocabulary of 400 basic English words so that they could overcome what was described as the language barrier and successfully complete the first grade of school. Tijerina believed that this basic skill of 400 English words would mean that they would not have to repeat first grade, fall behind their classmates, become discouraged or drop out at the alarming rate then prevalent among Mexican Americans in Texas public schools. The children were perceived to have a deficit (limited or no spoken English), and the aim of ensuring their success in school was laudable. But the children were neither mute nor stupid: they were fluent Spanish speakers. You might want to think about what message they were given about the lack of value given to their home language and – by implication – their culture (Guadalupe San Miguel 1987).

At the time that news of this project emerged, Bruner and his group of researchers were approached by Washington to address the 'deficit' issue in education. Bruner proposed a small research project. But such a small-scale offer did not suit those in power, and a few months later Head Start was started and aimed to be offered in every one of the states of the Union. The programmes which grew out of this and which are still in existence today provide grants to 'local public and private non-profit and for-profit agencies' (what we would call schools and settings) to provide comprehensive services which they call 'development services' to economically disadvantaged children and families, with a special focus on helping pre-schoolers develop the early reading and mathematical skills which some educators believe they need to be successful in school.

You can see how the programmes were based on the idea of there being a deficit in groups of children and were compensatory in nature. The very concept of 'deficit' made Bruner feel uncomfortable but he continued with the research. The findings of the research were important and showed that interaction and self-initiation were key factors in learning – or in the development of mind. In other words, to learn, children need to interact with others and to follow their own interests. But the notions of deficit and deprivation not only hung on but changed. Where deprivation had initially been seen as a consequence of poverty, a new idea grew – that of cultural deprivation. For Bruner, this had its root in the highly idealised middle-class view of what children – white, middle-class children – were and should be. It was a very Western version of the child who grows up in a nuclear family with a stay-at-home mum and a money-earning dad. The child is encouraged to play (i.e. to initiate activities) and to engage in constant interactions with the mother. Any family falling short of this was seen as deprived. Think about it in relation to your own family or the families of the children you work with or those represented in the books you have read. How many families conform to that model? Accompanying the Head Start program in the USA were many projects designed to teach mothers how to be more like 'good' or idealised middle-class mothers – i.e. to play with their children and to talk more to them and to allow them to sometimes take the lead. Later similar parent-education programmes were started in the UK. Some of the programmes did have some results in terms of turning children into those more likely to be like the idealised child and to succeed in school. But the negative effects of compensatory programmes often outweighed these small gains.

The important question now arises as to whether we can blame cultural deprivation for the failure of some children to thrive and succeed at school. Is it some deficit in particular cultures or is it some inadequacy in the dominant culture to recognise unfamiliar strengths and styles of being? Certainly, in the USA, the immediate response to the perceived and real failure of groups of children was blamed not on the child directly but on the mother of the child – or, more accurately, on the culture of the mother. It takes little imagination to realise that the mothers living in poverty in the USA were and still are primarily black or Hispanic, and the implication is that these cultures are wanting in some way. And here in the UK those families living in poverty may well be black or immigrant families, but they may also be working-class families. So here we have an added dimension of something to blame: class.

The Head Start programmes were well intentioned but stank of the condescension that often goes with reform movements. They continue to this day and state that they try to promote school readiness by enhancing the social and cognitive development of children through the provision of educational, health, nutritional, social and other services to enrolled children and families. In reality they ignore the key and painful question of what it is like to be poor, or to be poor and black or to be poor and Turkish or Afghani, or to be poor and black and Turkish or Afghani and have your children at a setting that promotes such an alien model of child-rearing.

At the time of its inception, Head Start was described as a programme that was affirmative, and in some senses it was. It genuinely wanted to improve the lot of the poorest children and possibly did some consciousness-raising around issues of poverty and difference. It is clear that some children have benefited from participating in the programmes in that fewer children from the programmes ended up with early pregnancies or going to prison or receiving welfare payments. But any programme that pays such scant attention to culture is bound to fail in the long term.

Setting expectations

There are examples of models of programmes which operate on the assumption that almost all children are competent and able to think and communicate and solve problems and develop. They are programmes based on higher expectations of children and that believe that our brilliant babies become brilliant toddlers and brilliant school pupils. They are not held back by an emphasis on basic skills but offer many possibilities for children to become engaged, involved, challenged and enchanted. Here are some examples.

- In his book *The Culture of Education* (1996), Bruner describes a project which he believes goes beyond the aims of Head Start by providing opportunities for children aged ten or eleven from poor communities and which does all the usual academic things such as raising achievement in reading and writing and other things but also makes children feel valued members of a community. The Oakland Project is a school in Oakland in

California and is at the hub of a consortium of schools spread throughout the country. On one of the days that Bruner visited the school the children were studying the after-effects of the oil spill in Alaska from the *Exxon Valdez,* and they were doing this in order to come up with a plan. Everyone could contribute a suggestion or idea, however wild or ill-considered. Someone suggested that you could take the oil off the wings of birds using peanut butter to blot it up. Every idea was seriously discussed. Nothing was laughed out of court. For Bruner, this was an egalitarian approach, and he described it as 'teaching by sharing' (1996: 77).

- Vivian Gussin Paley is an educationalist of great sensitivity and integrity. In her kindergarten classes the rules are often made by the children, but when one child's behaviour causes pain to another, Paley's rules come into play. One such rule is against the prevalent practice of children excluding others from their play or from their group. By talking to the children about this she ensures that the children actively explore the effects of their behaviour on others. You will often have seen this in practice where the children in the group of the insiders exclude the outsiders. Paley attempts to create a decent society within her classroom. There is little emphasis on basic skills; rather, the children play and talk and act and narrate as they explore how the world works and what their place in the world is.

> I have come to this classroom of three- and four-year-olds to uncover their secrets, but the children seldom reveal them in conversation. Instead, they change identities and burrow into hidden places: they speak in code and flee from invisible foes; they manufacture problems whose resolution depends on judgements I cannot anticipate. All year the fours have been announcing edicts for the containment of bad guys. Their rule-making is prodigious. Were I to impose prescripts at such a rate the children would withdraw in confusion, yet it is impossible for a child to suggest too many ... I record their fantasy play because it is the main repository for secret messages, the intuitive language with which children express their imagery and logic, their pleasure and curiosity, their ominous feelings and fears. For the price of keeping order in the room I am privileged to attend the daily performance of private drama and universal theater that is called a preschool classroom.
>
> (Paley 1988: vii)

We might call this teaching by narrative.

- In one of the famous baby and toddler centres in Reggio Emilia, the Pablo Picasso Infant–Toddler Centre, the children are fortunate to be in a green and leafy part of the city. In the playground, staff noticed that the children collected lots of found materials (things like stones and sticks and leaves) in order to make their playground look 'prettier'. They spent time looking at and exploring the cherry tree and were fascinated by a procession of ants. Emanuele said (about the cherries), 'My grandpa picks them and puts them in the basket ... and I eat them', and Aurora said, 'It's a doorbell, it rings where the ants live, there's a hill for the ants. They're here, they're here, they opened the door and here's the den for the ants, scratch to see if there's a little lizard too.' The staff recorded what the children said and kept photographs of what the children did. They were interested in what they called compositional research and chose to focus on the tracks and patterns the children made with the found objects in the playground. They decided to bring some of the same materials into the centre to see what happened. They added some man-made materials – pieces of metal or rubber or ceramics. They then noticed that the toddlers used strategies as they made groups and patterns and tracks. They noticed that the children used shape and colour, symmetry and correspondence, repetition and alignment and discontinuity. They charted the project in a little book called *We Write Shapes That Look Like a Book* (Cavallini 2008). What high expectations they have of these very young children and how well the children live up to them.

You may well be asking what this has to do with brilliant babies – the title of this chapter. It has to do with the importance of recognising that babies and young children, as active constructors of meaning, make sense not only of the world of objects but also of the world of people. And the adults who are with them need to pay careful attention to how they set about doing this. Through their interactions and their actions they come to an understanding that other people have minds too. They come to understand that peers and others have feelings and thoughts and ideas of their own, and what is fascinating is that they do this from a very young age. And it is worth considering whether this starts in infancy.

The infant as protagonist in the family drama

As we have said, children are born into a social and complex world and from infancy they are both participants or protagonists in this world. They can be the hero, the victim, the accomplice, the one in the right, the one in the wrong, the one who is blamed or the one who is praised. They may lead the action or follow the lead of others. The child, from very early on, learns to take on different roles within the drama of everyday family life. This takes place before the child is told to take part and before the child knows the rules that bind the actions. The child comes to discover through action what is allowed and what is not, what is possible and what is not. At first the child needs no spoken language in order to participate: the transformation of action into language comes later. As a member of a family, infants hears stories about their own actions from their parents or older siblings, and Bruner tells us that these follow what he calls 'the familiar Burkean pentad'. What he means by this is that all life can be seen as drama and that we can find out what the motives of the people in the drama (the children, the parents, the grandparents and so on) are by looking at their motivation in terms of two things: action (what they do) and discourse (what they say). The term was coined by Kenneth Burke in the context of theatre and drama, and he set up five questions (hence the word 'pentad') to be asked to try and uncover the motive. The questions are:

1. Who (or agent): Who is involved in the action and what are their roles?
2. What (or act): What actually happened? What is the action? What is going on?
3. Where and when (or scene): Where is this taking place? What is the background to it?
4. Why (or purpose): Why do the agents or those involved do what they do? What do they want?
5. How (or agency): How do those involved act? What do they actually do?

This is difficult to understand, but some vignettes might make the meaning clear. They are all drawn from Dunn's research.

- A twenty-one-month-old child spills milk and shows it to the mother.

  c: Look. Look. Look. Moon. There moon. Moon.
  m: Where's the moon?
  c: [inaudible] ... a moon. ... a moon. There sunshine.
  m: It's not! It's milk on the carpet. ...

  (Dunn 1988: 19)

  You can see how the mother makes verbal comments (or tells the story of what happened), and, as in all the examples cited by Dunn, these often refer to the cause or the consequences of what is clearly not acceptable behaviour by the child.
- This involves a child of three who is in the kitchen with her sibling while the mother is organising the cooking.

  m: Would you two like to go and wash your hands? ... Go and wash your hands, please.
  c: Why don't you wash your hands?
  m: Well, it's you two that are doing the cooking.

  Here the mother's response helps the child begin to understand the purpose of a rule (those who cook need clean hands). The child is questioning the application of the rule. She doesn't yet know that rules may sometimes apply to some people but not to others. The mother, by telling the story, helps the child understand.

(Dunn 1988: 35)

- Here the child is just twenty-eight months old, and she has overhead someone say that she has forgotten her pen.

    c: [to the observer] You forgot your pen. Forgot your pen ... could ... the other pen. Did you couldn't find your pen at home?

(Dunn 1988: 133)

Dunn's analysis is that the child is interested in the fact that adults and others make mistakes. She is very busy trying to make sense of the social world in which she lives.

These vignettes give striking examples of children actively making sense of all aspects of their lives. Dunn suggests that is it very likely that young children and infants need to learn to share their intention and feelings and to understand the social rules that bind their society together.

The implications for practice

1. *Bruner insists that we need to regard the human infant, from birth and possibly before, as being competent.* Those of us working with young children need to pay attention to the ways in which babies and toddlers give evidence of this competence. So we need to watch and notice what they are paying attention to. We need to take note of changes in their facial expressions, or their focus of attention, or their breathing rate, or any other physiological feature. Where possible we should take notes about what we see and hear and think about what they tell us. This can be both rewarding and revealing. It is certainly worth trying. Here are some observations from the developmental diaries made by parents (Karmiloff-Smith 1994).

    Dianne (three weeks): 'Whenever Jack and I are chatting, the baby seems to react. She stiffens her body a bit and looks in our direction – as if something important was happening. I've been reading about this sort of thing and it's true – she really reacts to our voices.'

(Karmiloff-Smith 1994: 39)

    Benji (ten weeks): 'He seems to watch my face a lot. But not just mine. When Raj picks him up, he fixes on his face too. Even when I take him out in the pram to the park, he watches people's faces when they look into his pram. He seems to find faces the most interesting thing, more than other things.'

(Karmiloff-Smith 1994: 42)

It is worth remembering that in the crèches or *asili nidi* in Reggio Emilia in Italy documenting the daily progress of the infants and toddlers is a recognised and valued custom. The staff there understand that working and student parents really appreciate receiving these daily portraits of the days of their children.

2. *Babies are not only competent, but they are communicative.* They spend an enormous amount of time in the first years of life interacting and communicating. Communication does not depend on spoken language but can be achieved through gestures, expression, sounds, body language and other means of exchange. We need to pay attention to the ways in which young children seek to communicate and respond appropriately. This sounds so sensible and straightforward but it is more complicated than it at first appears. Below are two identical episodes, one in which the mother responds appropriately and the other in which she responds in a less appropriate way. And you may well recognise yourself in the example of a less-than-helpful response. There is no implied criticism of the mother in either of the examples. She responds as best she can in her circumstances. The examples are merely offered in order to help you consider ways of responding.

> Oscar (fifteen weeks): Oscar has been put to bed. He is fed, warm, dry and healthy. Ten minutes later he starts screaming inconsolably. His mum goes into the room, picks him up, cuddles him and says, 'Oh, little boy! What is troubling you? Have you got a tummy ache? Shall I rub your little tummy to make it feel better?'

> Oscar (fifteen weeks): Oscar has been put to bed. He is fed, warm, dry and healthy. Ten minutes later he starts screaming inconsolably. His mum goes into the room, picks him up, cuddles him and says in an angry voice, 'Oh, not again! I can't cope with another change of bed linen!'

When children are already verbal, responding may be easier but in reality the adult response is often not focused on what it is the child is concerned with. This is more true of teachers and practitioners than parents. Exchanges that take place within the everyday context of home are more likely to be about a shared interest or event. What we as practitioners need to do is to try and respond to children in a way that shows we are attentive to what they are communicating about.

3. *Bruner tells us that infants and young children are hypothesis-makers.* This means that they ask themselves questions (not verbally at first) about the things and people they encounter. They question why things happen, how they happen, where they happen and so on. Those of us working with young children need to be aware of this implied questioning and use it as a means of understanding some of the behaviours that may seem random.

    Here are some examples to illustrate this. Please note that the comments in brackets are mine.

> Cameron (nine and a half months): He has a good look for a toy when he drops it. (His question might be 'where has it gone?') I give him a basket of toys when he's in his high chair and he picks them out one by one and drops them deliberately, then afterwards looks for them. (His questions might be 'Will they all fall to the ground? Will they all behave in the same way?')
>
> (Karmiloff-Smith 1994: 111)

> Harpreet (nearly twelve months): She loves being put in a large tub of water outdoors. Given two spoons, one solid and one with slits in it, she lifts each up and watches intently to see what happens. (Her question could be 'Why does the water come out of one and not the other?')
>
> (Personal observation)

> Laila (three years and two months): Laila loves moving things from one place to another. She gathers leaves and twigs in her little baskets and carries them from the garden to the hut and unpacks them. Then she goes out to gather more. Then she takes the things she has brought indoors and carries them all outdoors again. (Her questions are, perhaps, 'Can I fit all these things into this basket? Will they be the same inside as they are outside?)

Behaviour like this is often described with reference to the work of Piaget who talked of these repeated patterns of behaviour as schemas which were seen as evidence of thinking.

4. *Bruner is clear that cognitive development depends on two things: interaction and self-initiation.* We have talked about the implications for practice of interaction in the previous chapter. Self-initiation means allowing the infant or child to be in control of what to do, and this has important implications for our practice. In many settings a too-formal approach dominates, with children being required to do things (write their

names, count, sort objects, colour in pictures and so on). Children need opportunities to choose what to do and how to do it and who to do it with. In other words, children need be encouraged and enabled to follow their own interests in pursuit of answering their own hypotheses. They need to play.

5. Some of Bruner's early work was taken out of context and applied on a large scale in a well-intentioned but misdirected attempt to redress some of the inequalities in society. For Bruner, some of this was very destructive, and he was deeply concerned that *education and care programmes should not operate on a deficit model*. All children are individuals; all come from different backgrounds with different experiences, values, systems, beliefs, languages and cultures. Educators and practitioners should not make value judgments about any experience or culture. Such judgments can seriously impact negatively on the sense of self-worth of pupils and their families. Rather, practitioners should seek to know as much as possible about the experiences, languages and cultures of their pupils and offer opportunities for the children to build on that.

Looking back, looking ahead

In this chapter we have looked at Bruner's ideas arising from his interest in and study of babies. We started with a section examining his ideas about the competence of newborn infants and moved on to looking at one of the consequences of this work. Bruner's findings about the competence of infants led the government in the USA to start thinking about how some babies were 'deprived' and to find ways to compensate for this. That led us to look at the issue of expectations and how the expectations of educators and carers have direct consequences for children and families. We looked then at the infant as a role-player and a rule-maker within the immediate context of the family. The chapter ended with the implications of all this for our practice.

We now move on to start looking at the development and acquisition of spoken language.

Chapter 5

From communicating to talking

Introduction

In this chapter we start to examine Bruner's thinking about language itself, how infants acquire language and what roles others play in this. We will start by exploring Bruner's ideas about what cognitive skills children have before they acquire language that enable them to go on to acquire culture through language. We move on to looking at the ideas of Chomsky and others who provided some base from which Bruner's ideas developed. We then look at the vital role of others in language acquisition, particularly at the role of the mother or primary caregiver. And this takes us into the realm of rituals, routines, games and play. The chapter ends as all do with the implications of all of this for our practice.

Initial cognitive endowment

Bruner used the words 'initial cognitive endowment' to mean the skills, perception and problem-solving that laboratory tests suggest infants have that predispose them to be able to learn language. He is clear, however, that laboratory tests take place in a seemingly culture-free environment so must not be relied upon since culture and context are so essential to all human infants and their learning and development. He talks of four conclusions coming from this research and we will examine each in turn.

1. *Much of the cognitive processing that appears to operate in infancy does so in support of goal-directed behaviour.*

   Put simply, this is the evidence that human infants are actively seeking out regularities and patterns in the world around them and in this way are unlike the young of any other species. To illustrate this Bruner tells us the story of what he calls non-nutritive sucking, which means sucking not in order to obtain food. You will know that all mammals are equipped with processes to allow things such as initial feeding and attachment to a primary caregiver and sensory contact with the world.

He says these are all well buffered to prevent the infant from over-reacting. The baby sucks in order to take in milk but also sucks on a finger or a pacifier, which serve no nutritional purpose. This non-nutritive sucking buffers the infant because it relaxes muscle groups and keeps the infant calm. There is the possibility that this behaviour is hard-wired or inbuilt. But as soon as infants are a few weeks old they become able to control their sucking and to use it to meet their own goals as we saw in an earlier chapter where babies combined sucking with looking in order to improve the quality of an image. So a hard-wired behaviour becomes a goal-directed activity under the control of the baby. Papousek showed that babies of less than ten weeks in age could learn to turn their heads in order to turn on a flashing light array that attracted them. Their behaviour involved noticing a pattern, predicting what might happen, becoming habituated or used to and then bored with something and then changing their behaviour. Babies are able to coordinate actions in order to do something. We are back to brilliant babies.

2. *The second conclusion is the evidence that shows how much of the activity of the infant during the first year and a half of life is social and communicative.*

There is much evidence to show that the most powerful reinforcer of infant behaviour is a positive social response, for example a smile, a hug, a kiss or a positive comment. Conversely, the withholding of a social response can cause real distress and result in tears or tantrums. Within the first few months of life infants demonstrate both that they can mimic facial and other gestures and can also respond with stress if the mother wears a mask during feeding. If the mother or other carer playing with the child does not smile, the child is also more serious during the exchange. And there is laboratory evidence that the exchange between the primary caregiver and the child is, in effect, like a duet. Babies will respond to things such as changes in caregivers' heartbeats, or their tones of voice, or their facial expressions. In return, carers will respond to the babies' responses to them and so on.

3. *The third conclusion sounds very straightforward on first reading. It says that most of infant action takes place in constrained and familiar situations, primarily within the home, and that this action is characterised by being ordered and systematic.*

You will know that most infants spend much of their time in the safe and supportive atmosphere of the home and local community. You will also know that they spend most of their time doing a limited number of things. They eat and sleep and look and listen; then they reach out and hold and take and bang and drop. And repetition and practice seem to be routine behaviours. Here are some vignettes to help you recognise this behaviour.

- Mina tied a ribbon from her baby's foot to a mobile over the cot. When the baby kicked randomly at first the mobile moved. So she kicked again and again and again. After a while, Mina took the ribbon off the baby's foot with the baby watching her. The baby continued to kick despite getting no response from the mobile.
- Reza passed a plastic container from one hand to the other and back again over twenty turns. His eyes were fixed on the container as he did this.
- Isha throws everything onto the ground: a flower, a leaf, her bowl and spoon, her toy, her mother's scarf.

4. *The fourth conclusion is that the systematic behaviour of infants is extremely and surprisingly abstract.*

   Bruner suggests that the observed behaviour of infants in the first year of life demonstrates that they have invented rules for dealing with space and time and even causation. Here are some of the findings from research that support this:

   - When the baby is shown a moving object which changes its form behind a screen and emerges looking different, the baby shows surprise. The baby's rule? Objects should not change their form even when hidden from view.
   - When a remote-controlled car moves without anything visible to the baby causing this to happen the baby shows surprise. The baby's rule? Things can't move unless something moves them.

In his analysis, Bruner drew on the work of Piaget, who had talked about how children move towards logical thinking and as they do so look for things that are constant (or unchanging) and things that are not. Whilst doing this they *invent and apply rules* to explain what they notice. We have seen two infant rules in operation above: things keep their shape even if they are hidden from sight and things cannot move unaided. This making of rules is important to remember when you read what follows. One of the systems the infant encounters from birth is the *symbolic system of language, which is rule-bound*. This process of abstraction is the basis of infants forming hypotheses about the world and the people and objects in it.

So we have learned that laboratory or culture-free research shows:

- that infants are active constructors of reality;
- that they are intensely social;

- that their earliest actions and interactions are ordered and systematic and take place in familiar surroundings;
- that they engage in thinking which must be considered to be abstract in character.

Bruner's 'four endowments', which he calls means–end readiness, transactionality, systematicity and abstractness, are essential processes that aid the child's language acquisition (Bruner 1983b: 30). They don't give the child language but allow the child to build on non-linguistic experiences to generate the rules required for language. This is complex and the language is difficult to unpick, but if you read on you will find that you understand what Bruner was saying.

Learning a language: brilliant babies begin to talk

You will know that almost all babies within a year or so of life start using spoken language in order to communicate. In general, the exceptions are those babies who have some cognitive or auditory impairment that hinders or delays this. What we know is that human infants learn the vocabulary and the grammar of their first language or languages without the need for specific lessons or teaching. How this happens is still a matter of often fierce debate between different schools of thought and is something that interested and vexed Bruner.

He charted the thinking about language acquisition starting very long ago in the fourth century AD, with the writings of Saint Augustine, who based his views on his own experience and said that what happened when he learned language was that he would listen to the adults around him naming objects and when he did he would look at the objects, and, after hearing the words in different sentences, he gradually worked out what the words meant and said them. This is an interesting idea for someone writing so long ago (particularly since it clearly sees context being of some importance), but it will not take long for you to realise that it is a very limited explanation for an exceedingly complex process. It refers primarily to naming, to repetition and to imitation. This idea was popular for decades, and the most famous of its proponents was Skinner. Skinner, who was deeply scorned by Bruner, is sometimes described as seeing the child as the proverbial blank slate waiting to be written on by experience which was either rewarded or not. For him, the essence of learning was the reinforcement of a 'correct' response. The child, making an utterance that is perceived to be correct by the carer or parent, is rewarded with perhaps a hug or a smile: this has the effect of ensuring the child will make the same response on a subsequent occasion. You can see how limited an approach this is.

The main challenge to this simplistic view of language acquisition came from Noam Chomsky. He asked a whole set of new questions about how children acquire language, and it was these questions that prompted his new theory which, in itself, was complex and persuasive. He asked questions such as these:

- How do infants become able to combine words into new sentences which are comprehensible to others?
- How do infants become able to utter phrases or sentences that they have never heard before? If language acquisition is based largely on imitation, this should not be possible because no one the child has heard speak will ever have uttered these phrases or sentences. An example is, 'I seed it and I feeled it and it is not a dog.'
- Why do infants make errors relating to aspects of their language when they have never heard fluent speakers of the language make such errors?

Bruner tells us that Chomsky's answer to these questions was based on nativism, meaning that he believed that the mind produces ideas that are not derived from external sources. Chomsky was interested in the structure of language, and his theory was that the human infant is born with a device (a notional device, not something visible or palpable) that equips the infant to make sense of language. He called this the Language Acquisition Device (LAD) and said that its foundation was a universal grammar (what he called a linguistic deep structure) that humans know innately and not through learning. The child hearing (or later seeing) the language (the surface structure) is able to abstract the rules governing language and to generate the utterances possible in that language. It is important here to return to the notion of rules. All languages are rule-bound. In English, for example, the rule for making plurals for nouns is to add the letter /s/. But although this is a rule there are exceptions to the rule. Some words form plurals differently: think about the plural of 'child' ('children') or 'mouse' ('mice') or 'woman' ('women'). In English there is a rule relating to what happens to verbs when they refer to what has happened previously – i.e. to create the past tense. The rule is to add '-ed' to the verb, but again there are exceptions: think about the past tense of 'go' ('went') or 'see' ('saw') or 'fly' ('flew'). When children first start using plurals and the past tense they first use the correct form which they have heard adults use and which they are imitating. Then they use the incorrect form as they work out the rules they have generated and apply them universally. They say things that are not grammatically correct but follow the rules. They say things like 'The mouses goed into the hole.' You will realise that they will never have heard a fluent speaker of the language say that. It is what Chomsky called a 'novel utterance'. And this means that imitation alone cannot account for language acquisition. There are rules referring to word order, intonation patterns and many other things, all related directly to the particular language being acquired. English has fewer types of past tense than many other languages. The intonation patterns of Welsh are different from those of English. Mandarin is a tonal language whilst English is not. This is a fascinating area and one you can read much about.

For Bruner this was an extreme view but a very important one in that it freed a generation of those interested in the acquisition of language from the simpler explanations of Skinner. What it did do was to focus attention on rule learning and to open up possibilities for new theories. This was where Bruner himself stepped into the arena with his alternative or addition to the LAD, the Language Acquisition Support System (LASS).

Language Acquisition Support System

Bruner was concerned that Chomsky's system paid little if any attention to the importance of interaction in language acquisition. It is clear that the development of language involves negotiation between two people. For communication to take place there has to be a speaker and a listener, a shared topic of 'discussion' and the ability to attend or pay attention to what the other is doing and saying. Bruner thinks that in order for the child to be able to generate the rules of grammar there has to have been a history of social and conceptual experience. He argues that this experience must have taken place within routinised and familiar settings or what he calls *formats*. It is these very routines that make up his LASS.

Bruner put forward four ways in which his LASS can help the child move from prelinguistic to linguistic communication. We shall examine each of these.

1. It is within familiar and routinised formats that adults become able to highlight those features of the world that are known to the child and important to the child and that have a basic and simple grammatical form. A format is a predictable routine repetition of language.

    •   Lifting the child from sleep saying 'upsadaisy' or some other word or phrase routinely used to accompany this action.
    •   Saying 'Wave bye-bye to daddy/mummy' (or the equivalent in whatever is the child's first language) and waving whilst saying it.
    •   Saying something like 'Here comes the train' as the spoonful of food approaches the baby's mouth.

2. The adult helps the child by encouraging and modelling lexical and phrasal substitutes for familiar gestural and vocal means. This is what helps the children learn to ask or to master the request mode.

- The baby points to the banana on the table and makes a sound and the adult says 'Oh, so you want a banana do you?'
- The baby shakes his or her arms up and down in frustration and the adults say 'What do you want?'

3. Where the child has chosen what to do in play the child may operate in the pretend mode, which is a rich field for language learning and language use. The language children use in pretend play as they try out different roles is fascinating as they mimic the tones of voice, the inflections and intonations and the grammar and vocabulary of whoever it is they are 'being'.

> Four-year-old Barney, involved in role play, explores death and destruction. Here is what he says: 'Help, help! ... I'm destroying! The king! The invisible bad king! He told me to get you. If I don't he'll put glue all over me. I'm turning into a statue! Now I'm all chained up. I'm in glue prison' (Paley 1988: 118).

This is extraordinary use of language very unlikely to be heard in anything other than fantasy play.
4. When the primary caregiver and the child have had much experience of routinised formats they are able to generalise from one format to another. So they will jointly engage in activities that help the child use forms of words such as request (asking for something), the interrogative (asking questions), reference (talking about something) and so on.

For Bruner, formats were intimately related to scaffolding (which we discussed in the previous chapter). The formats provided a linguistic version of scaffolding within a routine or everyday and repeated task. Here the primary caregiver and the child *share an intention* to get something done with words. Before the child is able to do this the carer does it for her but as soon as the child becomes able the carer expects her to contribute. One of the formats that Bruner and his colleagues studied was reading. Here the caregiver is with the child looking at a picture book, with the adult reading the story or talking about the pictures and implicitly inviting the child to join in. Initially this book-sharing provides an opportunity for the child to reference or name. Reading proved a very stable routine. Bruner says:

> Each step of the way, the mother incorporated whatever competences the child had already developed – to be clued by pointing, to appreciate that sounds 'stood for' things and events, etc. The mother remained the constant throughout. Thereby she was his scaffold – calling his attention, making a query, providing an answering label if he lacked one, and confirming his offer of one, whatever it might be. As he gained

competence she would raise her criterion. Almost any vocalisation the child might offer at the start would be accepted. But each time the child came close to the standard form, she would hold out for it. What was changing was, of course, what the mother expected in response – and that, of course, was 'fine-tuned-by her "theory" of the child's capacities'.

(Bruner 1983: 171–2)

This is very important and detailed and gives a really clear picture of just how good teaching and scaffolding can work. It requires the sharing of attention, the child taking careful supported steps, the caregiver leading to start with passing control to the child, the caregiver adjusting his or her expectations of the child and having in his or her head an idea of the child's capacities. It is both fascinating and very important for us as practitioners. We have talked about expectations, and it will be obvious to you that someone who does not expect a child to be able to join in with reading will not invite the child to do so. Similarly, someone who expects a young child to be able to retell a story exactly or correctly may be in for a disappointment.

The significance of the daily routines in the lives of babies

In the lives of all infants there are certain things that need to be done to ensure that the infant is clean, dry, fed, rested and healthy. These cyclical repetitions of daily events with some changes and variations are what we are calling the daily routines. They can take place in the home of the baby or in a setting, and they seem to represent a significant step in the life of the child, allowing the child to form and maintain relationships with adults (parents or carers) and peers. Addessi, in her fascinating paper (2009), described an action-research project being undertaken by the University of Bologna, looking at how routines of the day enabled children to explore aspects of music as one of the possible communication systems available to them. Her work is influenced by the thoughts of Bruner, particularly on how formats or routines allow infants to come to understand cyclical time. It seems that the child pays attention to the repeated gestures and actions and sounds that take place during these repeated rituals. It is this that enables the child to anticipate and predict what has happened and what might have happened. Through interaction with an adult or a more experienced other in the ritual the infant becomes able to influence and regulate it. During the changing of a nappy, for example, there is a fixed routine, but this is accompanied by variation in terms of who changes the baby, what that person says or does, when it happens and so on. Addessi quotes the words of

Emiliani, who studied the daily lives of young children, paying particular attention to the repeated activities:

> The repetitive structuring of interactive sequences with the early forma-
> tion of routines that regulate and give order to the child's biological
> rhythms, aims toward the goal of survival, which can only be guaranteed
> by the organisation of social life on a daily level — the child must master
> it early on.
>
> (Emiliani 2002: 54)

Let us remind ourselves that Bruner defined formats as the repetitive sequence of the tutoring role of the adult through repeated activities. In other words, it is the actions of the adult in the routine interactions of the day that structure the spontaneous activity of the infant.

In her research project, Addessi observed the routine of nappy (or diaper) change. First, the mother and baby were observed, then the father and baby and finally both parents and baby. Be aware that this is a small scale piece of research, but the findings are fascinating.

They found that the ways in which the mother and father interacted with the baby varied, particularly in terms of the vocalisations used. The mothers tended to repeat syllables common in the language (Italian) like 'ta ta' or 'ba ba' and to respond to the baby's interventions or imitations. They tended to revert to the songs or rhymes within the culture. Fathers, by comparison, left more space between responses, allowing for some inventive sound-making, less rooted in the rhymes and songs of the culture. So the musical quality (in terms of range of pitch, timing, rhythm and timbre) of the parent con- tributed to the child's developing understanding of music. Most interesting was the fact that in the last session observed between father and infant, the two seemed to be perfectly attuned to one another and showed both antici- pation and synchrony. Their responses were described as playing together like two musicians. They kept their eyes fixed on one another as they vocalised, imitated and responded. Addessi says that the behaviour was not natural but co-constructed over time. This arose out of their shared and co-regulated actions day after day which allowed them to anticipate the gestures of the other and to adjust their responses. In Addessi's own words,

> This is precisely the function of routine, to construct the type of format
> or frames, allowing children to control time and its content, made up of
> gestures, emotions and actions ... Children can thus learn to vary
> and insert new elements, thereby developing their consciousness and
> co-constructing, in this case, through sounds, new knowledge on how
> to act.
>
> (Addessi 2009: 759)

Games

Bruner has always been interested in the evolution and nature of immaturity in a range of species. The period of human infancy is longer than that of other primates, and it is also characterised by a longer period of mother–infant interaction in what is called play between them. Bruner argues that this is initiated by mothers, and its aim is to entertain infants and to protect them from possible frustrations. Play, Bruner argues, protects the human infant from having to be inducted into community life too early. Play allows the infant to try out combinations of behaviour which might otherwise not be tried out at all but acted out in reality. One needs to view this with some caution since it could be said to perpetuate a rather Western view of childhood. Infants in the developing world also play with older children and with adults, and they play similar games where language is an essential element of the play itself. You will know some of these games from your own experience as a child or as a parent or as a carer. They are the sort of games where the adult and child in interaction repeat a sequence of actions, accompanied by spoken language, where something predictable but pleasurable happens. The ones we are most familiar with are games such as peek-a-boo and ride-a-cock-horse, and there is evidence that similar predictive games occur in almost all the languages of the world.

Bruner argues that games such as these offer the first occasions for the child to use language systematically with the adult and the first opportunity for the child to get something done with words. He describes the games as being idealised and self-contained formats. You can think about these game formats as having a deep structure and a set of rules, and it is these rules that allow the surface of the game to be managed. Let's analyse a peek-a-boo game where something is hidden and then reappears.

- The deep structure is the controlled disappearance and reappearance of the object or the person.
- The surface structure refers to all or any of the following: the screens or cloths or whatever is used to make the thing or person disappear and reappear; the timing of each act; the actual words or sounds used or the choice of what it is that is to disappear.
- The game is described as being 'non-natural': it is invented or made up, and it is tied together by the rules, which can be negotiated. Bruner calls these games idealised.
- The games are like language in that they involve turn-taking roles which are not fixed but can be changed. It does not matter who hides: there is always a hider and a hidden, an actor and an experience. Bruner calls these games little protoconversations.
- The games provide opportunities for spreading attention over an ordered sequence of events. So the game itself is the topic or the theme about which each of the moves can be seen as a comment.

If you are particularly interested in this theme of games you might want to read what Bruner has to say in his book *Child's Talk* (1983). He describes in detail the research he and colleagues carried out with two children called Richard and Jonathan. The two boys were observed once a fortnight, when their behaviour was observed and recorded. The work started when Richard was five months old and Jonathan was three months old. Here is one game which particularly fascinated Jonathan. It is a variety of an object disappearance and reappearance game.

- Jonathan and his mother first played this particular game when he was six months old and after he and his mother had played variations of the peek-a-boo game where the mother hid either her face or her little boy's face. In this new game, it was a toy clown that disappeared and then reappeared into and above a cloth cone. This was all accompanied by words: the mother asking, 'Who's this?' or 'He's gone! Where can he be?' Then a pause followed by 'Boo!' or 'Here he comes again.' The mother could vary the timing of each of the activities and use words to encourage prediction and heighten the excitement. What was unchanging was the deep structure: the appearance and disappearance of the clown. The game was observed over a period of about four months, and during this time several features changed. Jonathan started off by being an appreciative admirer. Then he began to predict. The mother then elaborated the language she used over time, and it was clear that the child used her utterances as cues for his attention or his involvement. As he became older, the mother's utterances sometimes reduced so that the reappearance was accompanied by just one word ('Boo!') and perhaps some warnings such as, 'Don't put that in your mouth!'

Jonathan's behaviour became more agent-like as he joined in, and by the age of about eight months he wanted to control the disappearance and reappearance and sometimes lost interest if he was not allowed to do so.

The implications for practice

It takes little thought to realise that since this chapter focuses on language acquisition it will be of most relevance to those working with babies and toddlers, although those of you working with slightly older children will also need to think about the possible significance of some of the ideas raised. We will focus our attention here on several factors, as follows:

1. *We need to consider how children work out the rules governing any system (such as language) or situation (such as a particular game) and how they then try implementing the rules and then either keep to them or change*

them. Practitioners will want to be alert to what it is the children are doing as they interact with adults or with peers. They will want to consider what it is the children are attending to and make their own guesses about what rules the children are positing. In essence this means being willing to believe that all babies are competent learners, equipped to use everything available to them – most importantly interaction – to develop their own hypotheses and generate rules.

2. *We need to be concerned with how children pay attention to the patterns they encounter in their experience and how they use these as the basis for generating rules.* There is some tendency in all adults to dismiss children's early behaviour and their early errors as signs of immaturity or lack of understanding. In essence, the mistakes children make offer us a window into their cognitive development. These errors (like those cited in this chapter relating to the overgeneralisation of rules relating to plurals or tenses) show us how hard children work to arrive at and use rules. What we see is that children first apply rules universally. They do this until their experience and interactions show them that one of the rules is that rules can be broken.

3. *We need to be sensitive to what significant adults do in repeated interactions with their babies in lifelike situations (bedtime, bath time, mealtimes) to scaffold learning.* We spend a lot of time talking about parents and in some situations trying to tell parents how to be 'good' parents. Many of the assumptions we make are that some parents are 'better' than others, and we base this, perhaps, on our own experience and on our education. What we should be doing is paying attention to how parents and carers interact with their own children, particularly during the routines and rituals at home. Many parents will have games and rituals of their own: others may not, and it is worth helping all parents understand that it is interaction (through talk, rhyme, chanting, songs, touch and expression) that is likely to be most helpful for the children to understand the world. This may mean making a small illustrated booklet (ensuring that it is available in the languages of the children in your group) which gives examples of some of the things parents and carers can do when they change the baby's nappy or feed the baby or sing the baby to sleep, together with a simple explanation of why this is important and how it helps the child learn to anticipate and predict. Interacting requires no special skill, no resources, no training. It requires only time and care. Do take care to reflect the home or out-of-setting experiences of all the children, including those whose languages and cultures are not yours.

4. *We need to ensure we highlight the significance of the daily routines and of predictive and repetitive games in learning.* Many day nurseries and settings which cater for babies are well aware of how significant the routines of the day are and know that they make up most of the experience of

young babies at the setting. It is vital that these are seen as important learning contexts and not just routines. So the interaction between you and the baby is highly significant. You will have read about some of the ways in which the practitioners at the famous crèches in Reggio Emilia make these real learning contexts by singing to the babies, placing mirrors over the changing table, playing music to the babies as they fall asleep and so on. Those of you working with slightly older children will already play predictive and repetitive games with them, and it is worth building up a collection that includes some of the games chanted or sung to the children in their first languages.

Looking back, looking ahead

In this chapter we have looked at Bruner's ideas about how children acquire language and have seen how he was influenced by the seminal work of Chomsky but felt that it lacked an essential element: the importance of the social, the contextual and the cultural in language learning. Language learning depends on the notion of the competent child, and Bruner cited the research evidence showing how goal-directed infants are in their attempts to communicate. The importance of children working out rules relating to the world and to language is essential to understanding his views on language learning. Bruner was extremely interested in the rituals or formats that occur in most families and which are often bathed in language. He believed these to be essential to learning language. These routines or formats can be seen as the precursors to games. The chapter ends with examining what has been learned and the implications for practice.

In this next chapter we turn our attention to how children, as they begin to use spoken language, learn how to name or refer to objects or people.

Chapter 6

Learning to name and reference

Introduction

In this chapter we continue examining Bruner's thoughts on language acquisition but now turn our attention to what he called 'the growth of reference' (Bruner 1983: 65). What this means is the development of the ability of learners to refer or draw attention to something that is of interest or relevance to them. 'Reference' is regarded as a somewhat outdated term but when Bruner was writing more than twenty years ago it was a well accepted term. We might find the more everyday word 'naming' more straightforward. Bruner, being inter-disciplinary in approach, started off his discussion in terms of a philosophical theory of reference, and we will start by looking at what he said about this. We then move on to issues more directly relevant: the management of joint attention, discussing the role of the mother or other adult in the use of spoken language for drawing attention to something (discourse labelling) and we then take a brief look at how the child achieves mastery of the rules of dialogue and discourse. For the first time we offer some critical views on Bruner's thinking about language acquisition. You are invited to consider where you stand on the issue. The chapter ends with examining the implications for practice.

Understanding a theory of reference

Bruner says that when we talk about reference we are talking about the development from one person trying to indicate some thought to another (perhaps crudely and immaturely) and what takes place between two people communicating where each is able to interpret what the other is saying. Based on his reading of the work of Hilary Putnam he says that four suppositions must hold true. These are:

1. *A person must be able to signal to another that they have something in their mind – a referential, in Bruner's terms.*

    - Evelina stares intently at a banana, back to her mother's face and again at the banana. Evelina wants to eat the banana. She is able to signal this desire to her mother. Her mother is able to interpret and understand the child's thought.

2. *This signalling can be very vague or very precise, and the two people involved in a dialogue may refer to the same thing but each have very different understandings.*

- When Chizzy was a very small girl her mother was talking about a unicorn and then noticed a look of surprise on Chizzy's face. 'What is it?' asked the mother. To which the child replied, 'Isn't that what Amy wears for school?'
- Francis (1983) cited the example of her own little boy whose comment 'Mine shooting gone', which he made as he and his sister sat eating biscuits, grabbed her attention. What could he mean? The mother, clearly attuned to her child's needs and interests and present during the exchange, worked out that he was telling his sister that he had finished eating his biscuit with the picture of a bow and arrow on it.

3. *All this must take place in the form of a social interaction which has to do with the sharing of attention.*

No example is necessary here, particularly in view of the fact that a whole section of this chapter will be devoted to discussing joint attention.

4. *The last is that there is some goal structure in referring.*

This is difficult to understand, but perhaps some explanation and examples will help. We human beings do not act in isolation. We are influenced by others, and this is so in homes and classrooms and settings. In all of these there is some level of reward embedded in the situation. This may be competitive, as where the learners are compared with one another; it maybe individualistic, in which the learners work for their own rewards; or it may be cooperative, where the learner works with others. It is more difficult to assign one of these to the sorts of interactions we are looking at. But look at the example below and see if you can see what each child's goals are.

- Williams (2004), in her wonderful piece about two siblings playing school in East London, cites the example of Wahida (the older sister) playing the role of teacher with Sayeda (her little sister).

Wahida: Now we're going to do homophones. Who knows what homophone is? No one? OK. I'll tell you one and then you're going to do some by yourself. Like watch. One watch is your time watch like 'What's the time?' watch; and another watch is 'I'm watching you. I can see you ... ' So, Sayeda, you wrote some in your book haven't you? Can you tell me some, please? Can you only give me three, please.

Sayeda: Oh. I wanted to give you five.

Wahida: No Sayeda, we haven't got enough time. We've only got five
          minutes to assembly.

Sayeda: Son is the opposite of daughter … and sun is … It shines on the
          sky so bright.

(Williams 2004: 63)

Sayeda, the less experienced other, is being inducted into the specific language and culture of school by her older sibling. Wahida, in the role of teacher, is able to demonstrate her understanding of school routines and language. She is scaffolding the learning through a routine which is very familiar to her although not to her sister. Neither has a goal that is clear although we might suggest that Wahida is rehearsing in order to consolidate her understanding of something in school. Sayeda is possibly engaged in the play because she wants to please her sister.

In essence, what we are talking about is how one person can manage to hold and direct the attention of another through the use of language. We have to operate on the assumption that the child, living in a social world that is full of the sounds of spoken language, develops some idea that these patterned sounds have meaning. They stand for and represent things. The things may be objects or people or places or groups of things or ideas.

- A child growing up in an English-speaking environment learns that the sounds (or the name) for the white liquid in her bottle is milk. An Italian child learns that this same thing is called *latte*. (The object in this example is milk.)
- The child learns that where there is one child we say 'child' but when there is more than one we say 'children'. More than one child forms a group, and the label for a group may be different from the label of an individual item.
- The child learns that there are many things that can be described as being red but there is only one person exactly like herself (unless, of course, she has an identical twin).

The power of pointing as a way of reference

Raymond Tallis has just published a fascinating book called *Michelangelo's Finger* (Tallis 2010). The cover of the book shows the pointing finger of God from Michelangelo's fresco in the Sistine Chapel. Tallis was Professor of Geriatric Medicine at the University of Manchester and is, in addition, a poet, a novelist and a philosopher. In this book he pays attention to the ability, unique to human beings, to point and analyses its significance.

The simple act of using the index finger to draw attention to something –
to point at it – implies some important things. It implies that the person
pointing (for us the child) understands that another person can share the space
within which the child and the desired object are located. Moreover, the other
person can see the child just as the child can see the other person. The child
has to appreciate that the other person, by following the pointing finger with
her eyes, is sharing attention on the object of interest. So now there is shared
visual attention. For Tallis this is the beginning of affirming that we live in
a shared world. In his words,

> Pointing is a fundamental action of world-sharing, of making a world-
> in-common. It not only tacks that common world together; it also expands
> it, and the two processes are not separate. When you are pointing to an object
> that I cannot see, and which is actually beyond the horizon of my visual field,
> you are affirming the existence of a world lying outside of what I can sense.
>
> (Tallis 2010: 132)

This might sound a little far-fetched until you think about a concrete
example. Imagine that you are in the park and you come across a woman
pointing to the sky. Around this woman is a group of other people all
looking upwards, straining to see whatever it is that the woman is pointing
to. You look up, convinced that there is something beyond your immediate
gaze, which will interest you.

For the human infant, however, pointing is overtaken by spoken language,
and then the world of shared attention through pointing is replaced by
shared attention through words. But it is important to consider just how
much infants have to know about themselves and others in order for them to
use pointing as a way of referencing.

We know there is evidence that primates are able to invite others to share
their focus of attention, but human beings are unique in being able to do
this using symbolic means: spoken words, signs, symbols, gestures, intonation
patterns, pointing and so on. We have spoken about how the infant starts to
pay attention to changes in the gaze of adults and begins to look in the
direction the adult is looking. We have seen how children begin to detect
the different meanings associated with changes in tone of voice or intonation
or facial expression. Their referential system, says Bruner, is a very open one.
It is important also to remember that for human beings context is essential.
In order to make and share meanings human beings use the context of any
exchange to provide essential cues. Bruner uses the unfamiliar term 'deixis',
drawn from linguistics, to explain this. Deixis refers to the phenomenon
whereby understanding the meaning of certain words and phrases in an
utterance requires contextual information. Words which have a fixed
semantic meaning, but which may also have a literal meaning that may

change depending on time and/or place, are said to be deictic. Thus, a word or phrase whose meaning requires this contextual information – for example, English pronouns – is said to be deictic. Pinker (1994) is helpful in explaining this rather complicated aspect of linguistics. He says that the main words which are context-dependent for making sense are the little words such as 'a' and 'the', 'here' and 'there', 'this' and 'that', 'me' and 'my', 'we' and 'you' and so on. And if you think about it you will almost certainly be able to call to mind examples of young children confusing these words.

Here is an example. The phrases 'killed a policeman' and 'killed the policeman' seem almost identical, but look at what happens when they are set in context:

- A policeman's fourteen-year-old son, apparently enraged after being disciplined for a bad grade, opened fire from his house, killing a policeman and wounding three people before he was shot dead.
- A policeman's fourteen-year-old son, apparently enraged after being disciplined for a bad grade, opened fire from his house, killing the policeman and wounding three people before he was shot dead.

(Pinker 1994: 76)

Identical accounts apart from the use of the indefinite article ('a') and the definite article ('the') and the context gives completely different meanings.

Managing joint attention

It is interesting to contemplate that Bruner was talking about the management of joint attention long before it became fashionable to do so. You may well be aware of recent work in the UK which identified good practice in early years education as being characterised by the provision of contexts allowing for practitioner and learner to have a shared focus of attention. It is said that the child and the adult or more experienced learner, when focused on the same thing, have a more meaningful interaction and that scaffolding is more effective. Bruner was, of course, thinking about the growth of reference and believed that it began early in life when the infant, in contact with the mother or other primary caregiver, made and sustained eye contact. What happens is that the mother or caregiver responds to this intense gazing by increased vocalisation and, shortly afterwards, by the child joining in. By the end of the second month of life this ritual of eye-to-eye contact plus vocal accompaniment has become well established. Mother and child begin to take turns, as though as one person stops the other takes over. This was all described by Daniel Stern in a paper presented to a conference in 1982 (Stern 1982).

Bruner's work built on that of Daniel Stern, who had analysed what happened when the mother (or other primary carer) started to introduce an object into the interaction with the infant in order to offer a visible or tangible target for sharing attention. In Bruner's own experiments he looked at what happened between Jonathan (you may remember him from an earlier chapter) at three months of age and his mother. She introduced objects in two ways. One was by putting the object between herself and the child whilst they were in eye-to-eye contact and moving the object to attract the child's attention whilst vocalising, saying something like 'See the pretty dolly' with a particular sing-song intonation. The other was to pick up an object to which the child was already paying attention and to move it into the space between them, again moving and vocalising as she did so. Bruner said that movement may be a way of grabbing the child's attention and ensuring that both are paying attention to the same thing. This he calls *object highlighting*. This type of behaviour drops out of the repertoire as the child begins to vocalise. By the end of the first year of life it has almost disappeared, and vocalisations become what Bruner calls 'place-holders' for the later and more sophisticated language that will develop. These are what Bruner calls *object-play formats*: a repeated action (or format) bathed in language.

Here is another example to consider. It refers to the work of Maire Logan Ryan (cited in Bruner 1983), who worked with dyads of mothers and their babies of about one year of age. The mothers were native speakers of Glaswegian English, and Ryan found that these mothers were more likely to use a rising intonation pattern when shifting reference to something other than what the baby was looking at. What was interesting was that the rising intonation pattern used by the mothers caused the babies to pay more attention to the object than the mother speaking normally. Bruner suggests that the first phase of managing shared attention is in the control of the mother. There are other experiments relating to children following the line of sight when the mother looks at a more distant object.

As babies get older they begin to point – first eye-pointing and later finger-pointing, and here it seems that the baby is the one controlling the shared focus of attention. So pointing plays a significant role in the developing child's sense of agency. Tomasello developed what he called the 'attention-mapping hypothesis' (Tomasello 1992). This held that the dyad of caregiver and baby engages in joint attention using a combination of two interactional styles and that these affect the learning of words in different ways. One is called attention-following (AF), which happens when the caregiver follows the child's focus of attention, and the other is called attention-switching (AS), where the caregiver switches the child's attention from the object the child had initially focused on to another object. The AS mode requires the infant to switch attention in order for both partners to be able to focus on the same thing. AF does not require this switch since the child is already focused on the shared object. Saxon and Reilly (1998) suggest that word learning is more likely to occur in AF mode since here it is the caregiver who names the object.

There is much more that you can read about this if it is of particular interest to you. It is important to understand this issue of intersubjectivity because it has enormous implications for all our work with children. You should know by now that intersubjectivity is the ability to understand the feelings and the motives of others and is something that our brilliant babies develop very early in life.

Language and power

Bruner has adopted a psycholinguistic view of language learning, which is surprising in view of his insistence on the importance of culture and context. Others, such as Basil Bernstein and Michel Foucault, offer a view which is more concerned with the *dialogic* nature of certain supportive learning environments (Inghilleri 2002) which promote the learning of language and take more account of the links between language and power.

Basil Bernstein was a significant figure in the early debates about language and education. He began his work in the 1950s and suggested that the ways in which children became able to use perception and reasoning were mediated by language. He believed that there were different ways of speaking (or what he called codes) and that these related directly to the social class of the speakers. So children coming from working-class homes experienced a particular style of discourse which was different from that of those coming from middle-class families. He called the code of working class families the restricted code and that of middle class families the elaborated code. As you can imagine, this view was unpopular because it was seen as offering a deficit model of the language of working-class children. Before you jump in to agree with this view you should know that Bernstein, like his fellow sociolinguists, saw language as a form of symbolic behaviour and was influenced by the work of Vygotsky. He was one of the first to see language as both a symboliser and a moderator of behaviour and also to recognise the importance of culture to language.

Critics of Bernstein were quick to see these as judgements rather than assessments. Let us look at these in more detail. A crude reading of Bernstein's work led some people to think that what he was saying was that the restricted code was inferior to the elaborated code. In effect, he was saying that the codes were developed in particular contexts and were shared by other speakers within those contexts and cultures. The elaborated code, however, had features that made it more suited to the requirements of formal education. The restricted code does not imply a limited or restricted vocabulary, nor does the elaborated code suggest the poetic or flowery use of language. What mattered about the distinction between the codes was what they were suited for. The restricted code was seen as being excellent in situations where there was a huge amount of shared, common-sense and taken-for-granted knowledge within the group of speakers. It was concise and economical and precise and was able to convey meanings in few words. Much might not be said directly but still be accessible to those sharing the culture.

Here is an example of each of the codes. Read them and see if you can say which is which.

- Thatcher has really done it this time!
- I saw Margaret Thatcher talking on television, and what she was saying about the miners made me feel certain that she plans to really break their strike this time. I think she is gunning for all trades unions.

The first example assumes that those listening share an understanding and perhaps an opinion of Margaret Thatcher, her history and her attitudes to the miners. So it draws on a store of shared meanings and background knowledge and carries with it the notion of talking as a member of a group. This is the restricted code. The second is the elaborated code, and it spells out everything in order that everybody can understand it. Higher education, in particular, requires students to be able to talk and write in ways which make things clear to those who don't share the speaker's or writer's history and experience. Speakers of the elaborated code can and do use the restricted code. The converse is not necessarily true.

Bernstein's work fell out of favour for many years, and it is only recently that it is being reassessed and given credence. It is interesting that in South Africa, fifteen years after the end of apartheid, children coming from the all-black township primary schools are failing at University, whilst those who were able to go to once-white town schools are not. Could Bernstein have an explanation for this in terms of what happened in the township schools? It is important to recognise that Bernstein did not cite the problem within the children, their families and communities and language: he cited the problem as being within the schools which did not seek to find ways to enable children to develop and use elaborated codes in certain contexts.

What was important about Bernstein's work was his recognition that issues of power affect language. He was interested in Vygostky's zone of proximal development (which was mentioned earlier in this book), and he saw it as a cognitive representation of the social world. He believed that the meanings and the cultural tools – books, words, symbolic systems – were subject to the different and unequal social regulations and attitudes to the knowledge to be transmitted or acquired. His main interest was in pedagogy, and it was here that he believed that educators could bring meanings to the child who might not otherwise have access to them or share them. You may be interested to know that Bruner was very influenced by the work of Basil Bernstein and also by Ivan Illyich. In 1970, he wrote an impassioned essay called 'Poverty and Childhood' in which he argued fiercely that educators should neither perpetuate nor institutionalise prejudice and social or racial inequality.

The implications for practice

McDonagh and McDonagh (1999) call a chapter they have written 'Learning to Talk, Talking to Learn', and this is precisely what should be at the back of our minds in our work with young children. The implications for practice here are straightforward but extremely important, and they all relate to aspects of shared attention. Bruner drew attention to how important the daily routines are in the lives of infants. This has now become accepted wisdom. Most settings appreciate that these recurring events throughout the day are important opportunities for learning. Bruner examined the literature on how mothers and caregivers, attuned to the infant's needs and interests, began to do some instinctive tutoring during these rituals. They watched the child's line of vision, looked out for a response from the child, bathed the task in language and set up a reciprocal relationship. Sometimes the child's focus became that of the caregiver; sometimes the caregiver's focus became that of the child. So, according to Bruner, the adult can provide a framework or scaffold that *enables the child to learn*. Arising from this there are a number of pointers for practitioners:

1. *We need to ensure that the activities we provide build on children's experience and that some of them are familiar and routinised. Within these activities the adults can cue the children's responses.* Think about the routines and rituals embedded in your day: story time, dinner time, circle time, nappy-changing, feeding, singing and so on.
2. *We need to ensure that we know as much as possible about the early language experience of the child in terms of the language or languages spoken at home, and we need to ensure that we make no judgements about the language or languages used.* We need to respect difference and avoid thinking of deficit.
3. *We need to enable young children to develop as speakers and listeners and to do this through modelling the forms and functions of language ourselves when we talk to the children individually and in groups. Moreover, we should ensure that our settings are buzzing with talk and encourage the children to ask questions and not only to answer them. We need to listen to the children as though we are interested in what they say.* It goes without saying that we need to be interested in what they are saying!
4. *We need to tell and read stories and invite children to tell their own stories and sometimes to enact them if they choose.*

5. *The activities we set up need to make sense to the children in that they have a clear purpose that is relevant to them and their interests.* In the best practice, activities are set up in response to the observed interests of the children. Think about some of your activities that might do this: sand and water play, building, cutting and sticking and other activities involved in making things, role and domestic and fantasy play, painting and drawing, singing and dance, story session, planting, cooking and more.

6. *We need to pay close attention to what it is about the activity that is of interest to the child and then get involved with the child around that.* This means that we have to hand control to the child and be prepared not to test the child through asking questions unless they are directly relevant to what the child is engaged with.

Looking back, looking ahead

In this chapter we have looked at how children learn to name things and refer to things. Although this sounds like something quite simple and straightforward, we have seen that it involves some complex under-standings – such as knowing that other people have ideas and minds and feelings, knowing that we share a world with other people, knowing that other people want to interact and communicate with us and having a range of expressive and communicative systems we can use: gesture, expression, intonation, body language, eye-pointing and pointing, in addition to spoken language. We have looked at how communication with another involves a shared focus of attention. Unless the infant or child and the adult or other person are focused on the same object or event or person there will be no communication.

We also touched on the troubled issue of language and power and saw how some of the work of Basil Bernstein in the 1950s tried to analyse what it was about language itself that caused certain groups not to succeed in school. Bernstein's ideas were found to be disturbing by some who perhaps read them too literally. The chapter again ended with the implications of what we have said for our practice.

In the next chapter we turn our attention to Bruner's ideas on how children learn to request and to question.

Chapter 7

Learning to ask and to question

Introduction

In this chapter we continue our examination of Bruner's ideas on language acquisition and move on from examining how children learn to reference (to name) to looking at children learning what Bruner calls 'request'. We examine what it is that the learner has to know about the patterns of asking questions or requesting something, and this implies that the child has to come to know something about the syntactic or grammatical rules about requesting as well as knowing something about changes in intonation patterns. We move on to looking at Bruner's three types of request:

1. a request for an object;
2. an invitation in terms of asking someone to join in;
3. a request for help.

It is important to remember that all aspects of the acquisition of language take place within a context, and we look at the child as apprentice in learning language at home and in her community and examine some of the research into joint attention and joint intention. We end the chapter by looking at the importance of children being effective questioners in terms of learning. In doing this we turn our attention to the provision in Reggio Emilia, with which Bruner continues to have close links.

Request for an object

Bruner tells us that asking for something or requesting is deeply embedded in context, and what he means by this is that whether we want to ask for anything from help or a service, to things, or information, or recognition, we have to take account of a number of things. We may need to consider the relationship of the child to the other person, the ways in which questions are framed within the culture of the child, what the child's intention is and where the exchange takes place. A request within the home will almost certainly be different in some ways from that within a more formal place such as the clinic or a classroom, for example. Bruner's own studies, as we know, focused primarily on mothers or caregivers with their children, and he noted that the earliest examples of request related to requests for a thing or an object. Let us look at some examples of children making a request for an object and see if we can work out what the person making the request (the child) has to work out about the person to whom the request is addressed:

- 'More dink' (drink): says sixteen-month-old Clarissa, asking her mother for a drink.
  Clarissa knows that her mother is the source of food and drink and knows that her mother will comply with the request.
- 'Give car': twenty-month-old Helmut asks his friend Rory for a car that both children are keen to play with.
  This is a request that may not succeed, perhaps because Helmut has far less of an emotional bond with his friend than he would have with his mother, his caregiver or his siblings. He does not know that his friend will comply with his request, partly because the car is something that both parties to the exchange want.
- 'Me cup': fifteen-month-old Ravi says this to his grandmother who hands him a cup, but when he shakes his head and repeats his request the grand-mother realises that what he is asking for is a specific cup – the one he likes best and to which he has attached the label 'me', possibly meaning 'my'.
- Ravi understands that his grandmother knows him well enough to allow him to refuse her first offer of a cup and that she loves him so will be keen to give him exactly what it is that he wants. Perhaps if he were in a setting he would have to modify his request because of the constraints operating in this more formal setting.

In a study carried out in the USA the question was asked about whether improving joint attention in settings described as offering low-quality child-care would enhance the language development of the young children. The researchers looked at forty-four childcare centres, all of whom agreed to parti-cipate. A member of staff from half of the centres was offered some training in how to improve joint attention in activities and then observed over time. The other centres, with no specific training, provided the control group. This is a small-scale piece of research, and it is, of course, dangerous to generalise from such studies, but the findings are interesting and possibly relevant. They found that training in how to offer joint-attention activities did have a positive effect on the language development of the toddlers (Rudd 2008).

It is worth stopping for a moment and thinking about how requests are framed in your particular language, family or community. In some families, some formality is required concerning what is regarded as polite behaviour, for example, saying please and thank you. In some communities, making eye contact is regarded as part of polite behaviour whereas in others this might be regarded as impolite. The caregiver is the one who inducts the child into the acceptable ways of asking for something. Here are some examples of this drawn both from personal experience and from Bruner's work.

- Do you really want this? Are you sure?
- Don't shout, please. Ask nicely.
- No, banging won't produce it.
- No, it's no use screaming. You've still got some on your plate, and when that is finished you can ask for more.
- What is it that you want? This book? No. This one?

Sometimes children indicate that they want something that is out of reach or that requires the physical intervention of an adult. The ways in which caregivers respond often turn into mini language 'lessons', as in Bruner's example where Richard asked for 'sos-man'. His mother replied 'No, not sos-man – saucepan with a "p" in the middle' (Bruner 1983: 101). Bruner's analysis is that it is responses such as these that move the child from being able to replace what we might call 'baby' words with real and recognisable words. As we have seen, children's requests provide fertile ground for caregivers being able to teach children not only about language but also about socially acceptable behaviour. For Bruner there are five important things that caregivers or mothers, in particular, can highlight when children ask for objects.

1. Requests must reflect *a real need for help*. Where they don't there is the opportunity to suggest to the child that she manage to do it alone or reach something herself.

    - 'You want that biscuit. Just stretch out and take it!'

2. *Times and routines of the day must be adhered to.* For example, when the child asks for a biscuit just before lunchtime or demands yet another drink after bedtime.

    - 'No, Rahua, not now. It is nearly teatime.'

3. *Requests must be reasonable and not demand too much effort from the caregiver.*

    - 'You want your book? It's in the other room and I am too tired to go and get it for you.'

4. *The help of the caregiver or adult must be appreciated and not taken for granted.*

    - 'You are such a good boy, Luka – saying thank you to me. You must know I am feeling very tired.'

5. *If and when caregivers just refuse to do something for the child they are implicitly expecting the child to accept their verbal reason for not doing so.*

- 'No, I am just too tired now' 'No, it's not your turn now.'

In the last example, the adult is inducting the child into the acceptable social rituals in the setting or classroom and doing that in response to a request from the child. So the request results in some learning about socially acceptable behaviour. Bruner reminds us that, 'Children learn to use language initially ... to get what they want, to play games, to stay connected with those on whom they are dependent. In doing so, they find the constraints that prevail in the culture around them embodied in their parents' restrictions and conventions' (Bruner 1983: 103).

Children interact with many people in addition to their parents, and all play a role in inducting children into the conventions of the language and of the culture. Parents induct children into the culture of the home; practitioners and teachers induct children into the culture of the school, the classroom or the setting. Bruner says that in these interactions (which he calls asymmetrical ones) adults are the agents of the child – they do what it is the child wants or needs.

Joint action: from shared attention to shared intention

We have thought about how very young children and adults – usually caregivers – become able to share a focus of attention through various communicative means – pointing, eye pointing, following the gaze of another, vocalisations and words. But something more complex happens over time. As the two engage in routines it is not only the attention that is shared but also the intention. We know that human behaviour is largely purposeful or, as Bruner would put it, goal-directed. As children develop and grow they become able to invite the adult to share their intention, and the converse is also true. Let us now think about this in terms of language acquisition. We have seen how children learn to name or reference objects and other people. We move on to examining how they become able to respond to questions and to ask questions. In order to be able to do this they need not only understand how the question is phrased but also the very conditions that underpin the question. Here, to illustrate this, is an example drawn from the work of Roger Brown (1973). He found that the mother of one of the infants he was studying, Adam, used questions in two different ways and it was examples of this that led him to think about what it was the child had to know in order to respond appropriately. Here are two such questions for you to think about. What do you think the mother is doing in each question? In what ways are they different?

1. Why don't you go and play with your ball now?
2. Why are you playing with your ball now?

In the first question, the mother is asking the child to do something: to go and play with the ball. It is a request for action. In the second the mother is asking for information. She is asking why the child is playing with the ball, and this is clearly a request for information. Adam's answers to these information questions usually started with the word 'Because ... ' He never started his replies to 'request for action' questions in this way. He must have been able to understand the purpose or the intention of the question. This is a complex act for a young children and another example of intersubjectivity. Without lessons the child has come to understand that one question which seems very similar to another (both being about the ball) are actually asked for different reasons.

Children as young as one to two years of age have already begun to engage in what is a uniquely human form of social cognition. They interact with others, sharing the focus of attention, and this requires them to make some kind of self/other comparison so that they can take on different perspectives in a shared task. Those of you familiar with the work of Piaget will know that he thought that very young children were egocentric and quite unable to see the world from any perspective other than theirs. Tomasello and Rakoczy (2003) dispute this and suggest that in the case of language, for example, children learn to use the linguistic symbols essential for sharing meaning and are able to play with words just as they play with objects. More than this, they suggest that children go from a simple participation in shared activities with a shared focus of attention with perhaps one significant adult to more complex shared collective intentionality where they begin to understand very abstract systems such as beliefs and values. Shared focus of attention, involving taking on the perspective of others is a stepping stone to this more abstract and complex understanding of culture. This is a serious and interesting point and worth taking time to think about. It links back to the writing of Tallis (2010), who, when talking about the act of pointing, was clear about how that indicated that even very young children have to know that they are neither alone nor at the centre of everything. They live in a world alongside others.

Requests happen in a parallel relationship where the child and caregiver are sharing a task or an action or an experience and the child then invites the caregiver to look at or to do something. The earliest invitations to joint action happen in the type of games we have already looked at where the adult and child jointly do something, and over time the child is both able to predict what will happen but also to invite the adult to start or to continue the game. Here are some examples:

• Hannah's mother played a game with her where she lifted up the baby's legs, held them up in the air, counted to three and dropped them again.

Hannah very quickly learned to lift her feet when her mother approached, clearly inviting her mother to play the game.

- Visito's sister invented a game to play with him when he was about six months old. She would bounce him on her knee, singing to him as she did so. The bouncing got faster and faster and the song louder and louder. The game ended when she put her legs straight out, making the baby bounce up and down as a result. At that point she held her breath and only when he had bounced up and down gave him a hug. After a while he would invite her to play the game by first grabbing her hand and shaking it up and down, then climbing up on her knee and finally shrieking the first line of the song.

Bruner suggests that the utterances made by young children when they invite someone to joint action are more sophisticated in some senses and simpler in others. The word 'more', you will not be surprised to learn, occurs frequently, and the child begins to use ingratiating phrases such as 'please, mummy', 'nice mummy' and so on. This ability of young children to recognise that their pleading is almost invariably successful in getting the adults to join in is staggering and shows just how much they understand about the minds of others. It is important to remember that since these joint actions are in the form of play they are formats and free of pressure. There is nothing for the child to get wrong. And the adult may choose to respond in a way that scaffolds the child's language learning by saying things like 'OK. Let's play the ride-a-cock-horse game' or 'I will draw the eyes and then you can draw the nose', but the essence of the game is in the pleasure of the joint action, the prediction and the outcome.

Requests for supportive action

Asking for help is something all children learn to do and involves a range of skills and understanding. Children are most likely to ask for help when they are involved in a goal-directed task. In other words, children are most likely to need help when they have set out to do something and encounter a problem or a difficulty. But asking for help involves more than being able to say the necessary words or make the essential gestures. It involves a huge conceptual leap in being able to recognise that in order to achieve their goal they need to do something or use something which is beyond their capability. They have to recognise that what they cannot do alone they will be able to do with help. And this, you might remember, is at the heart of scaffolding.

Bruner identified three kinds of requests for help, as follows:

1.   Translocational help (or help to get from one place to another, to be lifted up in order to see or reach something, help to climb up on something or get down from something). These are probably the

earliest requests that children make, and they do not necessarily require verbal requesting. Children can hold up their arms in order to be picked up or point to the windowsill on which they want to stand.

2. Precision assistance (or help getting something precise done, for example, opening a box, putting parts together, unscrewing a nut, winding up a musical box, taking off a lid and so on).

3. Power assistance (or the request for help where the child is too small or too light to achieve a physical goal – perhaps to carry a chair inside or open a door, for example).

In Bruner's studies he noted that children's first requests for this sort of help often related to children finding that they could not complete a task and then just handing it on to the adult to complete. Sometimes the request (initially in the form of handing the incomplete object to the adult) was accompanied by vocalisations, but not always. The child was often patient as the adult set to work and happily reclaimed the complete object when the adult had assembled it. With increased maturity the children began to pay attention to what it was the adult did in order to complete the task. Still later the child sometimes requested help whilst in the process of doing or making something. Here is part of a delightful episode where Richard, who is not yet two years old, asks for help from his mother. The request of help here is embedded in the action, and Richard's mother often needs his guidance in knowing what it is he needs. Richard starts by saying 'Mummy, Mummy' over and over again as he points to a cupboard which has one door open and one bolted shut. He then moves on to demanding 'up cupboard, up cupboard.'

Mother: What do you mean, 'up cupboard?'
Richard: Get up.
            [*Mother and observer laugh.*]
Richard: Cupboard, cupboard [*repeated several times*].
Mother: [*gets up, joins Richard beside cupboard*] I can't pick the cupboard up!
            [*Opens cupboard, talking softly to Richard.*]
Richard: [*stands, squirming, looking down. Looks into cupboard, spies a toy telephone*]
            Telephone.
Mother: How about these two telephones? You get out the telephone and make a telephone call. [*Starts to walk away; cupboard door swings shut again.*]
Richard: Mummy [*goes to mother, pulls her by the hand toward the cupboard*].
            Mummy get out telephone [*tries to reopen cupboard, then watches mother*].
Mother: [*props door open*] There we are! You get the telephone out then.
Richard: [*Reaches into cupboard*] Plates out [*excited*].

(Bruner, 1983b: 110–11)

You get a real sense of the struggle of both the child and the mother to communicate, but both persevere, and in the end Richard is able to take out the plates which he wanted in order to achieve his goal. He was briefly sidetracked by the telephone but managed to retain his focus and kept insisting on reopening the cupboard. Two months after this incident he was routinely and more successfully able to invite his mother to help him achieve his goal.

Apprentices at home and in the community

We know that children have been learning language from infancy. Their lives are bathed in language as they hear the everyday language of their homes and communities throughout the day – at mealtimes and bedtime, during clearing up and housework, out in the fields with a parent or carer, in front of the television, when their siblings play together, when the radio is on and so on. All of these are moments of language use and the potential for language learning. So the children can be regarded as apprentices within their homes and communities. They are watching and listening and learning, and practising and mimicking and absorbing and transforming and creating the ways in which words are used in all the social situations around and involving them. We need to remind ourselves that although this sounds rather random and haphazard, it is, in effect, very structured. Language is rule-bound and goal-seeking. We talk in order to make and share meaning, and we often adhere to the rules that bind our language together, and sometimes we break the rules. Rules not only relate to things such as how sentences can be made or which sounds we use but to more subtle things. Think about how there are rules within our own home or community about when to talk and when to be silent, who has more power and who less, what you can talk about and what not, who you can talk to about some things and not others. Here are some of the things a group of students said about the rules of language in their communities.

Mina: In my family we never, ever, ever talk about sex. If I mentioned it I would cause shock and consternation.
Alfie: In my family it's politics we aren't allowed to talk about. My dad gets a look of such anger on his face if I mention anything even vaguely political that I have learned not to do it.
Rashada: There is a real hierarchy in my family – very old-fashioned and sexist. My dad is seen to hold the wisdom, and he is the one who always talks first – sort of sets the scene. Then my older brother and then me and my sisters. I would never dream of introducing a new topic!
Indira: It is interesting because in my family we can talk about anything, but we are multilingual – all speak at least four languages – and some languages are used for some topics and other languages for others. I don't know where this comes from.

Much of the literature available to us about language acquisition relates to monolingual studies but we live in a multilingual world and in our schools and settings are many, many children who are not monolingual. Knowing something about bilingual language acquisition is important. There is little room here to go into this in any real detail but there is a recent and interesting, if very small-scale, research project examining the acquisition of two languages. Macrory (2007) looked at how one bilingual child constructed language, and in doing this explored the different rule systems of her two languages, French and English. Although Macrory had many possible research questions, the focus became that of examining the child's development of questions in both her languages. The child in question was a first-born child, a little girl called Adèle, who was looked after primarily by her French-speaking mother, who opted to stay at home with the child (in England) and speak French to her. The father was English-speaking and spoke to Adèle in English when he was at home. Adèle's mother only spoke English to her when her mother-in-law visited, since she spoke no French. The parents usually spoke to one another in English. The study started when Adèle was just over the age of two and was based on samples collected at monthly intervals. We will look at the examples of what the child learned about asking questions requiring 'yes' or 'no' answers in each language. In English, to ask a question that has a 'yes' or 'no' response the word order has to be inverted. For example, the sentence 'She is nice' has to be changed to 'Is she nice?' in order for a question to be asked. In French, a 'yes' or 'no' question can be asked in one of three ways. The first and second are by using the question marker *est-ce que* (literally meaning 'is it that?') together with a rising intonation pattern. The third is by inverting the verb and subject so that 'She eats' (*Elle mange*) becomes *mange-t-elle?* ('Does she eat?'). In French, the key feature of questions is the use of intonation. The researcher found that Adèle acquired her two languages separately in the same way in which monolingual speakers acquire their single language. Macrory also looked at the questions used by the child because this was what was providing much of the child's experience of asking questions in both languages. The mother, as a fluent French speaker and the more prominent of the models, almost always used intonation for questions. The father used more variation in his questioning, and Adèle had English input not only from her father but also from other people in her community. So her English input might well have been diluted by having other speakers as models. The major influence was clearly the mother, and this was shown where Adèle showed a preference for inverted questions in English and intonation only in French.

So here we see how a young child constructs her language through modelling her responses on those around her, and this offers support for the constructivist views rather than the nativist views. The child is not generating language in a vacuum but is an apprentice to skilled users in real and meaningful contexts.

Becoming a questioner

Bruner's model of the child as active learner, seeking to construct and share meaning seems to be a model of the hypothesising, questioning child. The child is constantly asking questions about the events, the objects, the people, the activities and the experiences she encounters. Before the acquisition of speech, the child's questions are only evident to us if we take the time and the trouble to try and work out what it is that the child is doing and why. Here are some observation notes for you to analyse in terms of what question or questions you think these very young children are raising:

- Theo (ten months): He copied me brushing my hair the other day, and now he brushes his hair with everything brush-like, including the broom and the nailbrush. When he saw me shaving my legs this morning, he tried to help using the spoon he was holding! (Karmiloff-Smith 1994: 185.)
- Bola (twenty-two months) collects leaves and puts them all in his small basket. He takes them indoors and then looks at each one intently and proceeds to sort them into three different piles.
- Evalina (eight months) sits in front of the mirror and touches her head over and over again. Then she touches her nose over and over again. Finally she closes her eyes, and when she opens them there is a look of surprise on her face.

We do not know the 'correct' answer when we ask ourselves what questions the children are raising, but we can certainly hazard a guess. Let us try doing this:

- Theo seems be asking questions such as 'What makes this thing [the hair-brush] good for putting in hair? Is it these things [bristles]? Would a broom work? Or a nailbrush? [Both have things in common with a hairbrush.] What is my mum doing to her legs? What is that thing she is using? Is it like a spoon?' The questions might relate to the purpose of the observed activities and the qualities of the objects involved. The child might be using comparison with known objects and is certainly paying close attention to details.
- Bola is doing something very familiar in young children. He is collecting objects from his environment and then sorting them out according to some or other criterion. He might be asking 'Are these all the same or are some different? Can I find all the big ones? Or all the small ones? Or the dark green ones? Or the ones with jagged edges?'
- Little Evalina in front of the mirror seems to be asking a whole range of questions. 'Is that me? Is that my hair? Is that my hand? What will happen when I move my hand? Is that my nose? Is that my hand again? What will happen when I close my eyes? Will I still be there?'

And here are some of the answers children give to questions they themselves have raised. They all come from the children in the infant and toddler centres or in the nurseries in Reggio Emilia.

- 'In the city, you need to have information so you know where to go; that's why they put up all the signs' (Reggio tutta 2001).
- 'Time is in the sky ... to see it you have to go up high' (Stefano, cited in Five and Six Year Old Children of the Fiastri and Rodari Preschools 2001: 39).
- 'We haven't seen the future yet – we'll see it when it comes. Tomorrow's future might be better than today's – it'll be sunnier and we'll go outside' (Omnia, cited in Five and Six Year Old Children of the Fiastri and Rodari Preschools 2001: 37).
- 'I'm a scientist when I discover that flies don't have hearts' (Alessia, cited in Five and Six Year Old Children of the Fiastri and Rodari Preschools 2001: 63).
- 'Columbus discovered America – he was a discoverer because he found it already made – but Archimedes invented machines that weren't there before' (Claudio, cited in Five and Six Year Old Children of the Fiastri and Rodari Preschools 2001: 63).

These wonderful extracts remind us that children are asking and answering questions all the time. They give clear evidence of being hypothesising children.

- In the first of these we find a child wondering why they have signs up all over the city and answering by doing a drawing of the signs and then telling an adult what the drawing shows.
- Stefano is thinking about time and trying to answer a really complex and abstract question about where time is and where you might have to go to see it.
- Omnia is thinking about what the future might be like and hypothesising that she will see it when it comes and that it will be better than the present.
- Alessia and Claudio are thinking about what a scientist does, and Claudio, thinking about what it means to discover something, makes a wonderful discovery of his own: that a scientist can discover something that already exists or invent something that has never been seen before.

Whilst Bruner tracked language acquisition in exquisite detail, he paid less attention to the significance of children becoming questioners as they moved from the home to the formal worlds of setting and school. He did, however, have enormous influence on those who set up and managed the famous pre-school settings in Reggio Emilia in Italy. He became a great friend and admirer of the city of Reggio Emilia and was even given honorary citizenship in 1998. This was at a time when his interest had shifted significantly from the individual child to the institutions of education. He said of Reggio Emilia that you have to understand a city itself in order to understand the educational provision within it. For him, Reggio Emilia can be described as a city neither too big nor too small and one characterised by what he called 'reciprocal respect' (Bruner 2004). For us, Reggio is a city of 160,000 people, 12 per cent of whom come from 120 different countries.

The pre-school provision is complex and made up of twenty *scuole materne*, thirteen *asili nidi*, twelve state preschools, twenty-one *scuole materne* and eleven cooperative infant–toddler groups and more provided by the local authority directly or indirectly in partnership with collectives. More than that it has become a body of knowledge and theory about the ongoing experiments in early years education and care. And Reggio is where the questions that children ask, explicitly and implicitly, are taken seriously.

We will consider this in more detail in the next chapter, where we move on to looking at Bruner's thoughts on pedagogy.

Implications for practice

1. For those of you working with the youngest children (babies and toddlers), the ongoing message is about *the importance of spoken language in all your interactions* with them. We have talked about the importance of speech in routines of the day, through games and songs and naming activities. You might now want to pay more attention to how children both respond to your questions and learn to question for themselves.

2. For all of us, *being aware of the child actively seeking to make and share meaning is essential*. It is only by really observing what children are doing, by listening to their utterances and by intuiting what it is that they are paying attention to, interested in and asking silent questions about that we are able to engage fully with them first on activities where there is shared attention and later where there is shared intention. In all probability you do much of this already, but *being conscious of what you are doing* means that you are more likely to use this as a pedagogic tool.

3. The *issues of shared or joint attention/intention* is a key and a fashionable one. We have seen how very young children come to acquire language and social/cultural skills and knowledge through interaction where they become able to focus on the same thing. We have touched on how older children can come to understand abstract things such as belief systems through interactions with others in their community. In schools and settings, this has been extended so the current focus is on what is called sustained shared thinking. This all arose out of the findings of the Effective Provision of Preschool Education (EPPE) Project (Sylva 2004) which highlighted this as a feature of good practice. *It is the interest of the child that is sustained and shared with another person – child or adult. Both have to be focused on the same task, objective or problem. The role of the practitioner or teacher is to try and manage this so that there are contexts to interest the children, to allow them to raise questions and to get involved. The genuine interest of the practitioner in what the children are doing is an essential feature of this practice, and there is advice on how to interact sensitively and positively.* It sounds so good on paper, so obvious. But

many questions are raised by this, and one of those is how it might be possible for the many, many children in our schools and settings whose experience is so different from that of the host, increasingly middle-class, culture of schools and settings. We will move on to this in the next chapter.

Looking back, looking ahead

In this chapter we have been looking at how children come to ask for help, for objects, for support, for attention and in order to enhance their growing understanding of their world. We, in the UK, place great emphasis on children answering questions and little on children asking questions, and yet there is much evidence that children do ask questions all the time and we have to be alert to this. We looked at Bruner's ideas on how the child learns to ask for an object and also at how the child, through interaction, learns to recognise and respond appropriately to different types of questions. We saw how culture-bound questioning itself is and how the adults can teach children not only about language itself but also about social conventions. We looked at the role of questioning in helping the child first share attention with someone else and then come to share intention with others. We paid some attention to children asking for help and saw how they operate as apprentices within the home and community and thus become questioners. The chapter ended with the implications of all of this for practice.

In the next chapter we turn our attention to Bruner's ideas about pedagogy.

Chapter 8

Pedagogy
Teaching and learning

Introduction

In this chapter we turn our attention to looking at aspects of pedagogy – the science or the art of teaching. In doing this we examine some of Bruner's thinking, much of it covered in his book of essays published in 1996, and then move on to exploring how some thinking has changed and is changing as new ideas are published and research discussed. We start by looking at what Bruner had to say about what he called folk pedagogy. We also look in more detail at the implications of his more recent focus on self-awareness in learning and look at this with regard to what was said earlier about sustained shared thinking. Then we turn our attention to his ideas on the curriculum, some of which were touched on earlier. We then consider some interesting research which examines differences between the practice of practitioners in the UK and those in Europe, particularly in terms of an emphasis on care.

Folk pedagogy

Bruner tended to use the term 'folk' where Vygotsky might have used the word 'everyday', and some people find this term difficult to accept because it carries with it some suggestion of prejudice against what could be described as the ordinary. When he talked of folk pedagogy he was talking about what we might call the 'received wisdom' about what children need to learn, what teachers need to teach, how this teaching should be done and so on. As you will know only too well fierce debates continue to rage about aspects of education. In this country we constantly talk about the effects of some of the current aspects of early years education – things such as testing young children, ranking schools, teaching to standards, the impact of our very early age of starting formal education and so on. All of these are based on what Bruner might call folk pedagogy.

When Bruner started writing there was an emerging view based on this folk pedagogy which held that children should be taught according to these lay or folk theories, which he described as being intuitive and based on concepts of children and childhood which he found very suspect – namely that children were wilful and hence needed discipline; that they were innocent and needed to be protected from the horrors of society; and that they were empty vessels waiting to be filled with the knowledge that only educators could provide. More than that, children were seen as being egocentric and in need of learning how to socialise. You might want to pause here to consider if you feel this attitude to children applies now, or applied to you when you were a child, and then to think about how it affected the way in which you were taught or in which children today are taught. Certainly in the media we read an enormous amount about how badly behaved children are, how inadequate many of their parents are and how society is falling apart. The impact this has on our current education system is apparent. But certain views have changed, and we now no longer see children as passive learners but as constructors of their own learning. We also see them as clearly situated in both social and cultural groups and are aware of the importance of interaction in learning. We understand more, if not enough and unevenly, about child development.

When Bruner was writing his initial thoughts on education he identified four dominant models of pedagogy as follows:

1. In the first *the learner is regarded as essentially an imitator, and the educator passes on skills and knowledge through the use of demonstration and modelling.* Bruner suggested that this approach celebrated talent and expertise as well as skills.
2. In the second model, *the learner is seen as being able to benefit from direct teaching. So learners are given the facts and rules of action and principles which they learn and then apply* – almost certainly in the context of an examination or a test.
3. The third view conceives of *the learners as thinkers, constructing and sharing meanings and learning through interactions with others and with the involvement of cultural tools (books, physical tools, symbolic systems and so on).* It places emphasis on collaboration and dialogue.
4. The final model is difficult to understand. It conceives of *learners as being conscious of their own knowledge learnt from their experience and beginning to consider more abstract learning held by the community – things such as beliefs, values and principles.* The role of the educator is to begin to help learners balance what they themselves know with what is known by the culture. We could say that this requires a balancing act for children between what they have learned and know and what others in their culture and community know and believe.

In summary, we can conceive of these models of pedagogy as being on a continuum ranging from the adult being totally in control to more modern theories which see children as active learners, learning through interaction and mediation, using cultural tools and capable of reflecting on their own learning. Aspects of many of these models might be seen in some of the nursery schools, nursery classes, children's centres and other settings for young children in existence today. And in some there are some serious and visible contradictions in the practice. For example, many early years theorists and practitioners believe our children start formal education too soon. They believe that young children need as much experience as possible of concrete, hands-on direct exploration before being faced with more abstract and often irrelevant tasks. They would like to be able to follow the child's interests and leads and not have to address the issue of testing these very young children against predetermined goals. You may well be one such practitioner.

Defining learning

The pedagogy adopted will largely depend on the definition of learning assumed. Bruner certainly did not see learning as a passive or an individual act. He saw learners as being situated in communities, and for him experience and culture were both very important. In his thinking about culture, mind and education he set out four principles or tenets that guided his psycho-cultural approach to education. These are:

1. The perspective tenet. In essence, this says that making meaning involves taking on board the perspective or the frame of reference in which the meaning was constructed, and it suggests that nothing can be culture-free. Everything that learners encounter is set within a cultural context, and learners themselves, although coming from a culture, may not be a mirror of that culture. *This tenet highlights the importance of individuals making meaning for themselves and being able to not only understand but also to create.*
2. The constraints tenet. Bruner believes that any form of making meaning is constrained in two ways. The first of these relates to the ways in which we have evolved as a species and our ways of thinking have evolved with us. The way in which we think now depends on and is constrained by what we thought previously. The second constraint is that our cultural tools – the symbolic systems we have developed within cultures – may not always be as useful to us as we need. *The implication for education is the need for learners to be equipped with the symbolic systems that will best serve their learning.*
3. The constructivist tenet. For Bruner this means that reality is not found but made. We construct meaning and, in sharing with others, may have to reconstruct it. Education must be about *equipping learners to use the tools for making meaning and building understanding and to help in the*

process of change in order to be able to adapt to changing conditions or circumstances.

4. The interactional tenet. For Bruner, the passing on of knowledge and skill involves what he calls a 'sub-community' in interaction. *Learners learn alongside others with whom they interact.*

It is this aspect of learning that we will focus on next.

Communities of practice

It is evident that when children or adults are learning something together they become more and more involved with one another as they jointly focus on something. If you have ever been involved with a group of children learning to play a piece of music, bake a cake, produce a play, build a tower or any other activity that requires collaboration and negotiation, you will have realised the power of the role of others in the process. The writers Jean Lave and Etienne Wenger (1991) talked of what they called '*communities of practice*' – a term not used by Jerome Bruner but clearly related to his ideas about learning. Wenger (1998) believed that these communities of practice were formed by people engaged in the process of collective learning in a shared domain of human endeavour. What he meant by that is clearly illustrated by some of his examples – a tribe learning to survive (hunter-gatherers out hunting), a troupe of artists working on a new form of expression (perhaps the Impressionists), a group of doctors exploring a new technique (possibly microsurgery) and so on. In these groups there are those who can be regarded as core members but others who are at the margins. Think about your own experience and you are bound to come up with an example where you were a core member of the group and other examples where you were clearly at the margins. Here are some examples.

- In a school production of *Hairspray*, one of the children missed the audition, which would have given her the possibility of becoming a core member of the group involved in singing, acting, dancing or making music. She overcame her disappointment by becoming a peripheral member as one of the stage hands.
- During class reading session, Deogratis, who was new to the country and had acquired no English yet, sat on the floor and organised books in piles according to size. Unable to be a full member of those who were reading to the teacher he chose to engage in a reading-related activity. We could say he was a peripheral member of the community of early readers.

For Wenger, three elements are crucial in distinguishing what makes a community of practice different from any other group or community. These elements are:

1. The *domain* which is the shared focus of attention. In order to be a core member of the group exploring microsurgery it is clear that you need to be committed to the domain (microsurgery) and have the competence, shared with others in the group. In one of the examples above Deogratis did not yet have the competence to be a reader in English.
2. The *community* is formed of those who focus on the domain and share the competence and engage in joint activities and discussions in order to help one another and share information. They are building relationships to assist learning.
3. The *practice* is what they do. You may well be an early years practitioner and if so, you share with others in the community of early practitioners a repertoire of what you do. This can be made up of the training and experience you have had, the difficulties you have faced and overcome, the rewards and successes you have enjoyed. When you go to meetings or training days you share practice and this requires sustained interaction.

Since we are all members of different communities of practice this is easy to understand. Let us move on to looking at the implications of this for pedagogy – for teaching and for learning. The model is clearly social: learning takes place alongside others and involves the making and sharing of meaning. Together the learners actively participate in constructing the practices of the group. When you think about this you might remember the work of Barbara Rogoff, who saw learners as apprentice thinkers. Lave and Wenger (1991) illustrated their theory by observing apprenticeships in the world of work – midwives, tailors, meat-cutters and those involved in Alcoholics Anonymous, for example. The child as learner looks, listens and observes before being drawn into being more active as a participant in some activity which has real meaning or consequence for the community. Think about children who play with dough whilst their mothers are baking, or children who tie their dolls to their backs just as the adult women in their community tie their babies to their backs. All of this involves identity, language and awareness of a continuously renewed set of relations. Some describe it as a relational view of both the learner and the learning and believe that it goes beyond experiential learning. What this means is that the child is learning from others as well as from the situation itself.

You might find it interesting to observe an area of your room and take careful note of what takes place there using the idea of communities of practice and Lave and Wenger's notion of 'legitimate peripheral participation'. This means looking at whether children are all able to access full membership of the group equally. In order to do this you would need to think about whether the child's prior experience helps or hinders her in getting engaged and being able to participate legitimately in the activity. Remember that in the early stages the child is an observer and a listener. As you continue reading keep in mind the child having English as an additional language or the child having recently arrived in the UK and think about how easy or difficult it is in your setting for such a child to be a core member.

Barron (2009) looked at the experiences of Punjabi children in a child-centred nursery class, set up in ways which we might all recognise and consider to represent good practice. The organisation of the day encouraged children's choice and independence, and the staff acted as facilitators of learning. During the day there were some times for focused activities requiring children to join a group in order to do more formal learning or to get involved in the routines and rituals of milk time or story time or fruit time and so on. The underlying influences could be said to be the interactive approach based on Bruner and Vygotsky but also the requirements and constraints of the Early Years Foundation Stage. It was assumed that learning would be social in the sense that children would learn from the adults and also from one another. Language was assumed to be essential for learning. This seems all very normal and to be expected. But let's think about what the activities on offer require in terms of prior experience. Let's think about whether the activities on offer genuinely make it possible for all children to become engaged. We will do this by taking a closer look at the nursery described.

There was a home corner which had a kitchen and a bedroom. Some of the equipment in the kitchen, at least, reflected what some of the Pakistani children might have encountered in their homes. The dolls were mainly reflective of a white indigenous culture in terms of their features and clothes. (Later, when the staff became more aware of Barron's focus, they introduced some more varied dolls.) The dressing-up clothes were reflective of Western roles and clothes. There was play with water and play with sand, and opportunities for painting including finger painting and hand painting. The role-play area changed over time and often offered themes unfamiliar to all but the small proportion of advantaged middle-class children in the group. During the time of the research it was initially set up as a travel agent offering skiing holidays in brochures and later as a greengrocer's shop. Do you think all children had an equal chance of being able to engage in all or any of these activities?

Barron's observations of what took place in the role-play area (the greengrocer's shop) show clearly that some of the language and the conventions this required clearly discriminated against some of the children. Based on the work of Lave and Wenger he saw the role-play area as having the potential to be a community of practice. The child shoppers and shopkeeper could be seen as apprentice real shoppers and shopkeepers. Here is an extract from Barron's observation notes:

- *Kelvin:*   Excuse me – what would you like to buy?
  Melanie: I'd like some carrots and toast – I don't need to buy all them things.
  Kelvin: You want some toast? There's no toast here!

> *[Adnaan comes and goes behind counter and helps himself]*
> Josh: *[to Adnaan]* Give *me* that bag – you've got to buy it!
> Adult: I know it's a British thing but it would be much easier if you would stand in a line.

(Barron 2009: 345)

The children of Pakistani origin came to the area and watched but appeared not to have the language or the skills to be able to join in, or, if they tried to do so, they just took the 'food' (as Adnaan did in the example) without asking for it. This upset the white indigenous children and the members of staff and so the Pakistani children became 'othered' or excluded. Barron adds that this is not because the Pakistani children have no experience of shopping but that their experience is built on different styles of interacting, of behaving, of being. They don't have experience of standing in a queue for food in a shop or of being in a shop that sells only fruit and vegetables. They also do not have the language to understand some of what happens, most clearly the comment made by an adult to the children, 'I know it's a British thing but it would be much easier if you would stand in a line.' Some of the Pakistani children might have been in shops where it was customary to pick up your milk or your DVD and take it to the counter, but this model (which might well have been familiar to some other children in the room) was not that promoted by the teacher. The teacher in this situation was very firmly in control although the activity was viewed as being open to being appropriated by the children.

What happened was that the Pakistani children were not admitted to the centre of the activity; they were on the periphery, and this must have had some effect on their self-images. They were excluded – seen to be not equal to the others – on the basis of their lack of the experience and skills and language required to be a full participant.

This finding is not new. Liz Brooker (2002) found something very similar when she examined what actually happened in a self-described 'child–centred' reception class. She found that many of the parents neither liked nor understood some of the things done in the name of education – going on outings, playing with sand or water, finger-painting and so on. These were not accepted in their culture and not part of their experience. They could not see how they contributed to the education of their children. The educators seem not to have been able to explain clearly to them what the children would gain from these activities. What is concerning is that schools and settings dismiss such concerns rather than really addressing them.

It is important for us as practitioners to remember that sometimes the things we take for granted are closely related to our own culture and our own experience and that we cannot generalise widely from this. What this means is that we need to ensure that we take parents with us by listening to what they say, taking their concerns seriously and being willing and able to explain to them why some of the things we do are regarded as important to children's learning and development.

The curriculum: what is taught

In any setting there is the predetermined curriculum (what the state or government has decided that all children should learn according to their age) and then there is the less apparent curriculum of what is given prominence, how the children are spoken to, what the expectations of the children are, what the resources are and what the preferences of the individual members of staff are. So there is an implied curriculum by which certain things are emphasised and others neglected. In some classrooms and settings we find boys dominating. A national curriculum implies that all children should be getting the same education but we all know that other factors play a very important part in determining what the school experience of individual children is. A child going to a Steiner nursery in a leafy suburb will have a very different experience from a child in a children's centre in an inner-city area. All this means is that it is not possible to regard any educational or care setting as being culture-free. The curriculum is about much more than the subjects on offer. Bruner argues that the chief subject matter of school, looked at culturally, is the school itself. What he means by this is that what the students experience is the whole act of being in the school or setting and this determines what meanings the student can bring to this. Let's look at some examples:

- Mrs Ramon, a bank teller from El Salvador, had moved to Canada with her children. Here is what she said about her child's experiences of school. 'In my country children say hello, good afternoon, how are you. Education is more than reading words ... the rules of courtesy are important for [schools] to impose. Here ... [children] don't even say hello to the teachers in the school, many times they just talk any way they want' (Bernhard 2004: 59).
- Abiola is concerned that her child is being discriminated against by the inflexible imposition of some of the rules of the nursery. One rule is that children should not hurt one another. Abiola thinks this is a good rule, and she encourages her three-year-old not to hurt anyone else. But a recent incident has caused concern. Two bigger boys started hitting her child, Bola, who responded by biting one of them, and this resulted in the nursery suspending her child. She feels that there might be an element of racism in this but also fears that Bola will start not wanting to return to the setting.
- Marina and Tonia are a lesbian couple who were looking for a setting for their small daughter. They visited several in the local community and spent time in the rooms, observing the ethos and the interactions and

eventually chose a school where there was an explicit anti-racist policy, many adults speaking community languages and a strong feeling of respecting individuality and culture.

You can see how in these examples there is something very important that goes beyond the subject matter. So the ethos, the attitudes, the expectations, the relationships and the interactions are a vital part of any curriculum and one that cannot be determined or managed nationally.

Bruner also believed that the educator or the practitioner has a vital role to play in stimulating the interest of the child in something new. Like Vygotsky he believed in the importance of the innate curiosity displayed by the human child but also saw the adult as a possible partner in any learning situation. We all enjoy what we get to be good at, and we may well give up on what we fail at. You will almost certainly be able to call to mind a child who gave up playing a musical instrument after failing a music exam or a child who gave up reading because of overhearing her mother say she was a bad reader. The message behind all of this is that it is not enough to wait for the child to show an interest in something but to introduce something to the child that is likely to interest her. Sometimes this is taken as suggesting that all children should do the same things at the same time. But this is not the message. The message is that the practitioner has a vital role to play in widening horizons, introducing new experiences, taking the child to new places. Here are some case studies:

- In the nursery schools in Reggio Emilia there is always an artist, crafts-person, mechanic or scientist working in a studio or an atelier. They are called *atelieriste*. The children are free to wander into the studio, to stand and watch, to question and talk to the *atelierista* and to select materials to make something of their own.
- In the wonderful music education being offered in the poorest neigh-bourhoods of Venezuela, children are given a musical instrument to play and are expected to look after it, to practise it and to give their time and attention to playing it in a group with other people.
- In a reception class in a school in Bath the teacher started a book-making project where parents of children were invited to come in and work alongside their child making a book about the life of the child. There were models of books made by other parents in previous years available to look at and read and a teacher available to support the work. At the end of a term the books were shown to the whole school during an assembly.
- In a children's centre in North London a 'life story' book was started for every child on admission. Once a week the books of three children were chosen to receive special attention during a story session at the end of the week. It was important that every child was recognised for some

achievement, however small. Children's books were chosen because the child had listened to a story, or helped another child, or drawn a lovely picture, or built something out of the blocks. After his turn, where the successful planting of a seed was celebrated, Wilhelm (aged four) announced to his father, 'I think now I can be a gardener just like you.'

More questions than answers

Bruner said that we should treat education for what it is, and for him what it was was political. He did not mean party political but political in the sense of being about how groups of people come to be able to make decisions about and for other people and the implications of that. You have only to think about how important qualifications are to getting jobs, earning money and having status, not only in our society but also much more widely. What makes education so special and so important is that it is the one institution that prepares the young to play a more active part in other institutions of the culture. So we have to look more closely at what we mean by culture. Bruner told us that cultures are not just collections of people sharing a history and language. Rather, they are made up of institutions (such as schools, hospitals, universities, libraries, banks, companies, shops, law courts, legal systems and more) where the roles that people can play are determined and where the respect accorded to these roles is worked out. In our society, doctors and lawyers are commonly held in high esteem: in some African countries healers and teachers are held in high esteem. Institutions are said to be responsible for many exchanges in society – things such as the wages that are paid for different types of work, the precedents that apply, the manners and statutes and language and thinking and sometimes even the uniforms or ideas of acceptable attire that are allotted. Many great thinkers have considered the roles of these institutions, including Pierre Bourdieu and Paulo Freire amongst others, and the debates go round and round. Should we have freedom of choice in terms of school for all children? But if people have to pay for a particular type of school or setting is this freedom of choice or only choice for the rich? Should we cream off the brightest pupils and have a meritocracy? Did comprehensive education really fail or was it never really tried? All of these questions are political.

Bruner, in his writing, keeps reminding us that we have always to keep in mind the ever-changing, often complex and always important concerns of the community we serve. How is the experience of children whose mothers have to go out to full-time work changed, and, if so, in what way? What effect does poverty have on children's learning and development? How do the children who come from other cultures sort out their loyalties and allegiances? How can we involve all the children in our care and education in all the activities and routines we offer? One way of doing it is to remember that classrooms and settings themselves are social communities, places where children can be supported or inhibited from coming to know this new world. To support the many children in our care who are in the initial stages of learning English or who are recovering from traumas that we cannot even imagine we need to take the time to observe them and listen to them. We also need to listen to their parents and carers and try and know as much as possible about the experiences that the children have had and will continue to have in their homes, their streets, their communities and their out of school activities. They can and will build on all of these.

A spiral curriculum

Fairly early in his career Bruner began to explore the idea of 'school' readiness or readiness for learning in the sense of what sort of learning a child could cope with. Piaget, as you may well know, thought of learning taking place through clear stages which he defined as being age-related and sequential so that children moved on from exploring things using movements and senses to eventually being able to reason and solve problems. Bruner's view was more nuanced and subtle but was definitely influenced by Piaget's ideas. Bruner believed that in teaching the teacher could start with an account or an activity which was well within the reach of the child and then go back to the same thing at a higher level as the child's abilities to think and reason developed. I think it is fair to say that the tone of his writing indicates that he was thinking of older children in formal settings rather than younger children, but we can learn from some of what he said. What he said was, 'Any subject can be taught to any child at any age in some form that is honest' (Bruner 1996: 119), and he then rephrased it to say that 'Readiness is not only born but made'. Now what he meant by this is that anything that someone decides a child should learn can be presented to the child in a way in which the child can make sense of. Initially the idea would perhaps be demonstrated and physical props used or movement and exploration be involved. Over time there would be less dependence on action and concrete exploration and more on abstraction and thought. In this way the instruction would move from the simple to the abstract. Let us try and take an example to illustrate this. We will look at three teachers' approaches to getting children interested in stories and books, starting with a teacher of three- and four-year-olds, then a teacher of seven-year-olds and finally a teacher of nine-year-olds.

- Marva has a group of three- and four-year-old children sitting with her as she reads them a story. She uses a large book, beautifully illustrated, and she ensures that all the children can see the book as she reads. She paces her reading, checking that the children are listening, and she uses different voices for the characters. When she has finished the reading she leaves the book out on a table together with some figures she has copied from the book and which are available to the children on a magnetic board so that they can retell and enact the story for themselves. She plans to read the same story again tomorrow. Her teaching is very much aimed at ensuring that the children can be drawn into the story and into the language of the story.

- Roberto is a storyteller who has been invited in to the class of the Year 2 teacher, Salama. She is concerned that the children in her class are not showing a great deal of interest in stories or books. Roberto is bilingual – he speaks Spanish and English – and there are several children in the class from Central America who are Spanish speakers. He decides to tell them a story but has the book from which he has taken the story to hand and plans to refer to it. It is also an enlarged text, and Roberto sets it out on an easel and proceeds to tell the story, first in English and then in Spanish. He is a skilled storyteller, and the children are quickly caught up in the story and wait at every moment of suspense to see what will happen next. They listen to the story respectfully in both languages. Then Roberto opens the book (which has both the Spanish and the English text in it) and invites the children one at a time to come and read a sentence in the child's language of choice. He has checked with the class teacher beforehand so he chooses children he knows will succeed. As each child finishes he rewards them with a smile or a nod and then asks the group a question getting them to think about the similarities and differences between the sounds or the features of the two languages.
- Nina teaches a Year 4 class, and she has started a book-making project. Each child in the room is making a book for his or her best friend. The work has been going on all term and has involved the children in listening to stories read aloud and in looking at books in the class, the school and the local library. The children have spent time talking in groups about what they think will make a good book, and they have interviewed their best friends to find out what sort of books they like. They have been told they must know what language their best friend likes to read in. So they are exploring genre, style, taste, difference and language. The children can clearly only write the book in their first language, but the children in the local secondary school who speak some of the community languages have been drafted in to try and translate the books.

You can see how a topic like becoming a reader (and a writer) can be introduced in different ways according to the abilities and interests of the children and how the practitioner or teacher can adapt the ways in which the topic is introduced so that they become more complex and more abstract. To succeed in school it is obvious that learners must become able to deal with symbolic systems and abstract ideas. To be able to do this successfully we would argue that they need much experience of exploring the world physically before they are able to move on to being able to do this using symbolic systems and abstract thought involving memory.

Social pedagogy

The term 'social pedagogy' is used to describe what adults can do to promote personal development, social education and the overall well-being of the child alongside parents or when children are in early years settings or schools. The adults involved are expected to play parenting/caring roles to try and meet the needs of what is called 'the whole child'. You can see that this approach to pedagogy goes beyond the notion of children having to be taught a subject-based curriculum. It involves helping children come to understand systems of beliefs and values.

The term is widely used in Europe and those involved may be childcare practitioners, social workers or child-protection officers, and in the training of these professionals there may well be a course called 'social pedagogy'. You will find social pedagogues in Germany, Norway, Denmark, Sweden, Finland and Iceland. In the UK the term is only just coming to be used, and this comes about primarily because of a growing concern about a number of issues presenting in schools and settings – things such as bullying, truancy, school refusal, child abuse and more. In 2008, the Department for Children, Schools and Families set up an expert group to review the roles of all those involved with children. The group has yet to report back (Kyriacou 2009).

Pat Petrie (2005) identifies the social pedagogue as a practitioner concerned with the development of the whole child and hence involved in all aspects of development and learning. She believes that any place where children are cared for and educated extends the focus beyond the academic to encompass all aspects of learning and development.

Cameron (2007) believes that the UK should consider introducing social pedagogues into the system but feels there are two major barriers to this happening: first, the low status accorded to children, child-rearing and child welfare in England and second the emphasis on accrediting performance rather than valuing critical enquiry.

It is clear that Bruner did not mention social pedagogy, but he would certainly support the idea of a move from a pedagogy focused on testing children to one that promoted more thinking and questioning. There is little doubt that he would have supported any intervention promoting the social, cultural and emotional development of children.

The implications for practice

You may have found this a rather difficult chapter to read because it sometimes deals with things that you may not regard as being directly relevant to your thinking about education and care. And you may have read through it with a feeling that you can learn little from it. But it will probably not surprise you that there are more implications for practice drawn from this chapter than any of the others and that is because this chapter is about teaching and learning in the broadest senses.

1. As always, we are reminded that *we need to always see the child as an active learner, involved in social and cultural groups, trying to make and share meaning through collaboration and dialogue*. So we need to ensure that in our settings children are encouraged to play and work with others and to engage, whenever possible, in dialogue. The implications for those children who have little English is to try and ensure that there are older children or adults around who can interpret and intercede for them when possible.

2. It is important to *consider how you define learning and then to check whether the opportunities and activities and support and interactions you provide match that definition*. If not, perhaps something needs to change. For example, if you are required to keep to a formal school timetable that breaks the day up into short sessions but you believe that young children need long unbroken stretches of time in order to get deeply involved, you might try talking to your manager or head teacher, giving clearly thought-out reasons for your request.

3. *Children need opportunities to be creative* – to question and think for themselves and to seek answers and do things in their own way. Think about whether completing a worksheet offers any opportunities for being original or creative or whether it promotes a model of being just conformist and doing what you are told.

4. *Children need access to relevant symbolic systems.* They clearly need to be drawn into the alphabetic system and rules of English, but they can best do that if they are also allowed to draw on and show off about the systems they may be more familiar with. You may have read the work of Charmian Kenner where she talks of how bilingual children teach their peers about the features and rules of their first language (Kenner 2010).

5. We cannot just respond to what the children bring. We need, of course, to know what experiences children have had and build opportunities for them to use these as the basis for further exploration and understanding. But *we need also to take a lead in introducing children to new things and new experiences*. Perhaps we will take them on outings to new places or invite in theatre groups, artists, storytellers, musicians or craftspeople to entertain and enchant them. We will read them stories about real and possible worlds. We seek to tempt them to try new things and discover what it is that they can do.

6. *All children need access to the appropriate cultural tools to be able to use these to make sense of their world, to be able to understand and adapt to change.* This means that children need to be able to draw on their previous experience, which means that practitioners need to know as much as possible about what the child has done and still does out of the school or setting so that the events that take place in the setting do not make the child feel like an outsider. This is a very difficult thing to do but it is important to keep considering it.

7. *The work on communities of practice is relevant to us because it reminds us that we engage the children in activities or 'work' and they can be seen as apprentices*

in this process. To begin with this apprenticeship is likely to involve them in looking and listening. Later, as they are drawn into the community of practice they begin to play a more active role and use language. Again, this is difficult to manage where there are speakers of languages other than English and does suggest that work needs to be done with parents, trying to find out what they want and expect from the setting and to explain why we do the things that seem not related to 'learning' things such as the use of sand, water, play, paint, outings and so on. We cannot take for granted that all parents will understand or appreciate how hard children are working when they seem to be 'just' playing, and it is important that we learn how to explain why and how children's learning and development is enhanced by these things.

8. *It is important to think about why education is political* and to consider what this means for you as a practitioner, for the parents whose children you care for and educate and for the children themselves. Where judgements are made that affect the lives of some groups, this is unfair. Where access to resources is not equal for all groups, this is unfair. Where people who work together don't share common pay and conditions of work, this may be unfair. There is probably not much you can do about these things, but knowing about them will make you more able to feel a part of the setting as a community. It will help to keep in mind the needs and concerns of the families of the children in your care.

9. There are things we can learn from the work done on the training and use of social pedagogues in other countries in Europe. We can learn the importance of having someone in the school or setting who has *responsibility for overseeing the well-being of the whole child* and whose role might include *reminding other staff members that education is about more than the written and assessed curriculum: it is about the personal, emotional, social, cultural and aesthetic as well as about the cognitive.*

10. *The spiral curriculum helps us consider how we match the activities on offer to the abilities, interests and perhaps the ages of the children.* Younger children need a curriculum that encourages them to make meaning and share meaning. They should have access to exploring numbers of things using whatever they have available for this exploration: touching, dropping, pulling, looking, listening, mouthing, tasting, smelling, pushing, throwing and so on. They need to be able to do this alongside others with whom they will interact. As children get older they will become able to use memory and engage in activities that depend on this as they act out what they have seen, try possible roles, explore what happens if … and so on.

Looking back, looking ahead

In this, the longest chapter in the book, we have looked at a range of aspects relating to Bruner's ideas about pedagogy – about how and what is taught by the practitioners and about what is felt and experienced by the children. We started by looking at Bruner's criticisms of what he called folk pedagogy, and that led us to consider how we might define learning and how our definition of it might then inform our practice. That led us on to thinking about the ideas of how those learning together on some shared topic or theme form a community of practice, which is something entirely positive for those accepted into this community but isolating for those not drawn fully into it. We then thought about the curriculum – not only the written and sometimes national curriculum but also the unintended or hidden curriculum which can be so powerful in shaping children's motivation, self-esteem and confidence. A large section of the chapter was devoted to how we can provide activities which will lead children to raise and ask and then attempt to answer questions. For Bruner and for us this is a key feature of successful early pedagogy. We then looked at two other issues: Bruner's spiral curriculum, where he asserted that a topic can be introduced in appropriate ways for children of different ages and revisited again and again in appropriate ways as children's learning becomes more abstract, internalised and complex. We touched on how the idea of social pedagogues – those involved in attending to the well-being of the whole child – might fit well into early years practice. The chapter ended with a list of the implications for practice arising out of all of this.

The next chapter, the last in the book, is devoted to the work Bruner did over many years around the importance of narrative to learning.

Chapter 9

Narrative

The making of stories

Introduction

In this chapter we turn our attention to Bruner's more recent work where his preoccupation has been how we use the making of stories to interpret, explain and understand the world. In his book called *Making Stories: Law, Literature, Life* (2002) he looked beneath the stories we tell in order to make sense of our lives and examined the moral, ethical and psychological problems that underpin them. He was considering how narrative, which, as we have said, is a way of interpreting and explaining our lives, can be used as a tool in a number of disciplines – the ones listed in the subtitle of Bruner's book (law and literature) and also anthropology. In this chapter we will explore several themes, including the reasons for narrative and how it works; the nature of narrative and its uses; why story and not something else; narrative in the lives of children; and narrative, cognition and the self.

Narrative and how it works

For the past two decades Bruner has been systematically developing what some call a narrative view of culture and mind and has argued that reality is itself narratively constructed. His interest in narrative started when he was teaching two seminars on narrative at the same time – one to a group of psychologists and the other to a group of writers of narrative (i.e. poets, novelists, critics, editors and playwrights). Both groups were interested in psychological and narrative questions as well as in readers and writers and texts. But there were differences between the starting points and the analysis of the two groups. The psychologists worked in a manner Bruner called 'top-down', whilst the writers worked from the 'bottom up', and what he meant by this was that the psychologists approached narrative by thinking about its relationship to mind and cognition and looked at story in terms of its ability to explain something. In a sense they approached narrative in the same way a scientist approaches a problem to be solved – looking for patterns, and answers. For Bruner, this way of working (which he calls logico-scientific or paradigmatic) ignored the context. The writers, starting from the bottom up, worked very differently. They took a particular narrative, poem, story or chapter and examined it for evidence of what the author was trying to say. This made their approach more bound to culture and context. They read the text in search of its meaning.

The nature of narrative and its uses

According to Bruner, there are two reasons for looking closely at just what narrative is and at how it works. The first, he believed, is to control or sanitise the effect it can have in something such as psychiatry where a patient who is ill is helped to tell the 'right kinds' of stories in order to be regarded as well. Virginia Axline (1964) wrote a powerful and moving account of a five-year-old boy called Dibs, who was said to have a very high IQ but who was quite unable to relate to others or control his fears and anger. Axline charted how, through a slow and painful process involving play therapy and talk over a long period of time, the child came to be able tell the 'right' kind of stories. He had been brought to the clinic by his parents who found him difficult to handle and said that his teacher could not deal with the little boy's physical attacks on others and his inability to be a social member of the class. In one of his play-therapy sessions, after a year of telling frightening and tragic stories, he told Axline this:

> 'Birds come there in that tree and I open my window and I talk to them. I send them around the world to different places. I tell them to go to California or London or Rome and sing songs and make people happy. I love the birds. We are friends ... But right now I have some-thing else I must do. I must get my sister out of the box and decide what to do with her. She has to stay at home. And when the father comes home from his office he scolds her. Then the sister goes to live with the pigs. And so does the mother'. He laughs. 'Not really ... They live together in a house. The mother, the father, the sister and the boy.' He picked up the little boy he had designated as Dibs and the grown-up Dibs figure. He held them both in his hands. 'Here is little Dibs and grown up Dibs ... This me and this is me.'
>
> (Axline 1964: 178)

You can see how, in this deeply moving extract, the child reveals aspects of the unacceptable stories he had been making (about his sister and the pigs, for example) but also displays that he knows what an acceptable story is. This is what Bruner would regard as narrative being used to determine the mental health of the child through the child's own 'version' of reality.

The second reason for studying narrative, according to Bruner, is to understand the relationship it has to reality, to see it as a mirror of real life and to explore what it tells us about human beings and their motives, their feelings and desires, their expectations and dreams. When you think about narrative you will realise that although stories may be initially deeply rooted in real life and real culture, they often go beyond the real to the possible. Think of some of the great stories that you have read or heard – *Alice in Wonderland*, *The Lion, the Witch and the Wardrobe*, *The Wizard of Oz*, the Harry Potter stories and hosts more. Writers clearly draw on reality or on their own interpretations of reality. They recreate aspects of their world and their culture and in doing this enable those who read or hear the narratives to come to understand some universals (things such as love, hate, jealousy, fear, anger, sibling rivalry, envy, desire and so on). These universals can be applied to not only real worlds but to imagined worlds, good or bad. So our narratives encompass autobiography, biography, novels, romances, fantasy, science fiction and fact.

One of the things that makes us special as a species is our ability to understand the minds, feelings, intentions, motives and desires of others. You have encountered this concept of intersubjectivity earlier in this book. Tomasello (1999) argues that it is this – our capacity for intersubjectivity – that makes us able to live a collective life within a culture. Bruner adds to this his suggestion that this collective life is only possible because we are able to organise and communicate experience through narrative. His thesis is that it is this organisation of our experience, needs, desires and motives that converts our unique individual experience into what he calls 'collective coin' which we can share with others. The writer draws us into a world which may be quite unfamiliar to us but which embeds sufficient aspects of universality in the text to allow us to arrive at conclusions, even when things are suggested or implied rather than stated directly. Here is an example. It comes from the wonderful and only novel written by Arundhati Roy called *The God of Small Things*: 'As a child she had learned very quickly to disregard the Father Bear Mother Bear stories she was given to read. In her version, Father Bear beat Mother Bear with brass vases. Mother Bear suffered those beatings with mute resignation' (Roy 1998: 180). Using only forty words Roy takes the reader into the early experiences of a child who has witnessed abuse. Little more needs to be said for us to feel the child's pain. We do not have to have experienced abuse ourselves to understand this. Think carefully about this and about what it tells us. We can help children deal with some of the most difficult issues in their lives through the reading, telling, making and enacting of stories. This has enormous implications for our curriculum and the way in which we organise our time and activities.

Legal stories and narratives from anthropology: the significance of thick description

Creating a narrative is not by any means confined to the world of the made-up. Narratives appear in many aspects of life, including in the law courts.

A legal story is the story that is told before a court. It has two tellers. First there is the narrative that tells what one party alleges that another party has done – an act that is in violation of the law or statutes of the county or country. Then there is the narrative of the accused party who seeks to defend his or her position by claiming either that the alleged act did not take place or that he or she played no part in it. The court then has to choose between the two stories (supported, of course, by evidence and legal processes) and make a judgment. In essence, the jury must decide which story is true, legitimate, acceptable and supported by evidence. Bruner goes to great lengths to discuss what makes a story into a legal story but we will not go into that here. Rather, we will look at Bruner's idea about culture being essential to understanding narrative. We will turn to literature again, for an example.

This time we look at Harper Lee's famous book, *To Kill a Mockingbird,* set in the Deep South with its entrenched intolerance, prejudice and racism. In the narrative the hero, Atticus Finch, is the white, liberal, anti-racist lawyer and father of two small children. A black man, Tom Robinson, is accused of raping a white woman, and Atticus Finch defends this man in court.

The chosen extract comes from the court after Tom has been asked by the prosecuting counsel, Mr Gilmer, what he was doing on the land of the alleged victim, Miss Ewell. In Tom's response he refers to the fact that he was doing some chores for her. As you read it pay attention to the tone of the lawyer and the things he doesn't quite say but implies.

'Why were you so anxious to do that woman's chores?'
Tom Robinson hesitated, searching for an answer. 'Looked like she didn't have nobody to help her, like I says –'
'With Mr Ewell and seven children on the place, boy?'
'Well, I says it looked like they never help her none –'
'You did all this chopping and work from sheer goodness, boy?'
'Tried to help her, I says.'
Mr Gilmer smiled grimly at the jury. 'You're a mighty good fellow, it seems – did all this for not one penny?'
'Yes suh. I felt right sorry for her, she seemed to try more'n the rest of 'em –'
'You felt sorry for her, you felt sorry for her?' Mr Gilmer seemed ready to rise to the ceiling.
The witness realised his mistake and shifted uncomfortably in the chair. But the damage was done.

(Lee 1960: 201)

The context of the Deep South and the culture of prejudice and discrimination is evident in the language used by Gilmer and leads to the inevitable conclusion of the case. (If you have not read the book perhaps this will tempt you to do so.)

Mattingly et al. (2008) tell us that not only is Bruner's focus on narrative being cultural but also culture being narrative. So people tell a narrative that was there before them and which they are helped to understand by the elders in the community. In Bruner's words:

> It is as if we walk on stage into a play whose enactment is already in progress – a play whose somewhat open plot determines what parts we may play and toward what denouements we may be heading. Others on stage already have a sense of what the play is about, enough of a sense to make negotiations with the newcomer possible.
>
> (Bruner 1990: 34)

We don't create any story from scratch, in a vacuum. Rather, we draw on the stories and rituals and rites of our own cultures and build on those.

In the field of anthropology, the ways in which the lives and cultures of people are described involve more than mere observation. They involve what the famous anthropologist Clifford Geertz called *'thick description'*, and by this he meant that the observations are not only about what researchers see and hear but that they also, crucially, involve their own interpretation of what they see and hear. Geertz says that 'What we call our data are really our own constructions of other people's constructions of what they and their compatriots are up to' (1973: 9). Geertz is one of the anthropologists described as being an interpretive anthropologist. To illustrate this more clearly we look at a research project carried out by a group of researchers coming from the UK, Canada, Thailand and Italy. They were concerned with trying to find a methodology for a truly cultural study of development and learning in early childhood. They called their project 'A Day in the Life', and what they set out to do was to film a day in the life of one two-and-a-half-year-old girl in each of five different cultures: Peru, Italy, Canada, Thailand and the UK. The investigators then viewed the films, selected clips were made and combined in a tape, and this was then offered to local investigators and to the child's family. The reflections of these people were also taped, and then all the material was examined to gain an appreciation of the child in a cultural context. The work is fascinating and a good example of thick description. It is thick because it consists of one layer of description or interpretation built upon another layer of interpretation. Here are some snippets from Gillen (2007) to consider

> In their attempts to paint a picture of the child and her interactions within a cultural context the researchers included a session where they took the compilation film to the family and they then filmed the interview with the family as they discussed what they had seen. One of the questions the researchers asked local investigators to focus on was the family's view of what is meant by the 'strong child', which is, as you may know, one of the themes of the Early Years Foundation Stage in

England. The family were asked for their own most appropriate positive adjective for their own child and within their own culture. In Canada the mother suggested that her child should be sturdy, by which she meant to be kind, independent and sociable. In Italy, the father highlighted the importance of the role of parents for the child's well-being and for the child to become *uno bambino in gamba* (meaning a caring, sharing, powerful, independent person) and said that they were able to give the child 'our good principles' (Gillen 2007: 212).

In Thailand the family wanted the child to be confident, obedient, to stay with the family and be self-reliant, and in Peru an aunt, grandfather and parents felt that each played a vital role and emphasised the importance of traditional values. In the UK, the mother felt her children (twins) were both their own selves and stressed the impact of the environment which she felt contributed to their differences.

A narrative from the South

Hasina Ebrahim (2008) has written an interesting and relevant article examining ethical ways to involve children as participants in a research project. The work was carried out in two early childhood settings in KwaZulu Natal in South Africa. The settings served very different communities, reminders of the apartheid divisions in society. Centre A was a middle-class private setting in what had been a white area. It was well resourced through the fees paid by parents and racially integrated. Ten children from this site were involved in the study, aged from two to four years of age: five boys and five girls. Centre B was a site on the outskirts of a town and was a poorly resourced, community-based setting in what had been an African area. It received a small subsidy from the Department of Social Development, and it was part of a programme looking at the impact of HIV/AIDS and other barriers to learning. The area was desperately poor; disease was rife as was crime. Eight children from this site were involved, aged between four and six – four boys and five girls.

In order to carry out the research Ebrahim sought the consent of the adults concerned. In Centre A it was clear that parents were self-confident in their self-appointed roles as advocates for their children. Any refusal for child participation came from the white parents. They were anxious that the fees they were paying would be wasted if time was used up by the research. Some were sceptical of suggestions that their children had anything worth sharing with the researchers. One African parent was worried about her child's relative lack of competence in English but was reassured when it became clear that older isiZulu speaking children would act as interpreters. Some of the Indian parents were impressed that Ebrahim was carrying out the work as part of her doctoral thesis.

At Centre B, access to the community was needed since this was a community project, and this was negotiated through involving political and traditional leaders, parents and non-governmental organisations working in the area. The members consulted were very eager to support the approach, thinking that it might not only give information about the participation of the children but also offer some opportunity for additional improvements to be made to the setting. This was, of course, beyond the scope of the research. To contact parents and carers was more difficult because of the possibility of illiteracy and the desire not to exclude any on this basis. One biological mother and eight grandmothers attended the meeting (they were carers owing to the deaths or absence of the mothers). No refusal was given for the participation of the children, and Ebrahim suggested that this was because the setting was seen as a place of hope, learning and safety in the context of deprivation surrounding it. In light of what many of the children had witnessed in their short lives, participation in this project was seen as a soft option.

Ebrahim wrote more about the participation of the children in the project and explained how the use of thick description allowed her to analyse what was observed. She said that she took note not only of what the children said and did but also of their gestures, facial expressions, posture and behaviour. She observed the children involved in physical activities such as running and jumping, doing drawings, creating a wall of photographs and telling stories. She says, 'Young children tell stories to construct a sense of self, to become part of a culture, make sense of the world, to solve problems, to deal with feelings and to form relationships' (Ebrahim 2008: 7). It seemed obvious that examining the children's narratives would be a fruitful way of understanding their views of their world but certain things emerged for her: there should be no fixed idea of what made a story – no beginning, middle or end. The stories that emerged included some extremely moving stories told by the children at Centre B when the children talked about illness, loss, death and sorrow. The children at Centre A told stories about babies and relationships and knowledge of big school and what was good for girls and good for boys.

Narrative in the lives of children

Bruner tells us that children enter the world of narrative early in life. Those of us who have children or who have spent time with children will find this no surprise. Almost as soon as children begin to use spoken language they combine what words they have together with facial expression and gesture and intonation into tiny proto-narratives. Here are some examples.

- The child looks at her empty ice-cream cone and says, in a mournful tone of voice, 'All gone!' (The child tells the sad story of how she has eaten all the ice cream so that now there is none left.)
- Arturo, given a present on his birthday, beams and says *ammi me* (*ammi* is what he calls his aunt). (Arturo tells the happy story that his aunt has given him a present and he is happy.)

The urge to make sense of experience through story seems to arise from the child's earliest conversations with adults within the context of the culture. You will have read something about this earlier in the book. In these exchanges it seems that the adult's intention can be seen to be narrative in the sense of turning any exchange into a story to help the infant make sense of it. One clear example of this comes from the work of Catherine Snow (1977), who, in her analysis of the speech used by mothers even in the first few months of life, noted that they commented on everyday events in a remarkably narrative way, imputing motives and emotions and the rudiments of a plot. Here are some examples supplied by students.

- My husband laughed at me when I asked the baby, 'Where's it gone?' when she dropped the rattle. He asks me if think the baby knows what has happened to the rattle and if she can tell me this.
- My mum says I am ridiculous when I say things like, 'I know what you are smiling at!' or 'Take that grumpy look off your face.' She says it is as though I think the child knows more than she does.

Gordon Wells offered the example of a child called Mark, just short of his second birthday, who engaged in a real conversation with his mother, taking turns and being able to comment on what the birds were doing outside his window. The conversation started with Mark drawing his mother's attention to the birds and his mother then asking him what they were doing. His answer was intelligible only to his mother: 'Jubs bread.' (*Jubs* was his word for 'birds'). Wells tells us that two weeks later he was involved in an extended conversation with his mother and as they talked about an imagined shopping trip he gradually took over the role of principal narrator (Wells 1981).

Bruner (2002) himself wrote about what he called the narrative precocity of infants and in doing this he cited the studies of the tape recordings of Emmy's musings to herself in bed before she fell asleep. The tapes were all recorded before Emmy reached the age of three. In his wonderfully entitled paper with Joan Lucariello '*Monologues as Narrative Recreation of the World*' (1989) he showed how this small child used narrative. In his later book he discussed some surprising findings. For example, Emmy talked not only about the routines of the day but seemed to be very attracted by and interested in something strange or unexpected that had happened. She then mused on how she had perhaps dealt with similar things in the past or how she would deal with them if they should happen again. Bruner concluded that she was so intent on getting her story right that she seemed to have a narrative sensibility that enabled her to look for and often find the correct syntactic forms. So Bruner suggested we may have a predisposition to tell stories in order to make sense of reality.

The reason children become narrators is because they explore the expectations they have developed about how the world should be. They develop these expectations through their experiences and their interactions and the ways in which they look for patterns and regularities in the world. But they also love the unexpected, the fantastic and the surprise. Think back to what you read earlier in this book about the games of suspense and prediction that adults play with children and recall how pleasurable these are for the children. In the stories they tell there is often an aspect of the unexpected, the unusual, playfulness with which they view and explore the world. Here are some examples of narratives told or written by young children in which the strange or the fantastic mingle with the ordinary and everyday.

- The first was told by four-year-old Octavia. It is a beautiful example of a child mixing book language and everyday language in a tiny narrative.

  'Once upon a time when I was little in my garden, there were a earth-worm coming out of my plant.'

- The second is written by Sam when she was five years old:

  This is a witch who has caught a clown and she has stuck a knife into the clown. She mixes the magic powder to kill the funny clown. She is killing him just because he is funny. But there was reason why she is going to kill the funny clown because she doesn't like funny things and all clowns are funny and specially that one. Every one like him but that witch. Even the other witches loved him dearly. They all thought he was great except for that one who was the only witch in the wild world who didn't like funny things. She really did hate funny things ...

- And this is written by Peter when he was seven years old. It is called 'The Boy who Broke his Laser Beam':

  Long ago, before motor cars were invented, there was this little boy and his name was John. This boy named John liked to go in the forest to see his grandparents and on this particular day he was walking through the forest when, just when he walked through a clearing of four trees, a giant net sprang on to him. The next thing he knew was that he was flying to a nearby cave in the claws of a bat ...

- Claudio made up a story about the witch's ball. It goes like this:

  The future can only be seen in the witch's ball. We can't see it: I don't know if I am going to be good tomorrow! To know that you have to study, to think with your head. The future is tomorrow, 'cause the glass ball shows you what there'll be tomorrow or what there was before. Witches are made like us, but they've only got one tooth – they're born like that. Now they're all dead but the glass balls are still here and that's where we can see the future.
  (Five and Six Year Old Children of the Fiastri and
  Rodari Preschools 2001: 46)

The narrative creation of self

Bruner says that although researchers and philosophers have traditionally linked thought with reason this is not necessarily inevitable. There is another way of thinking and that is the thinking that goes into storytelling or narrative. One particular kind of story is the story of one's own life: the autobiography. For Bruner this can be seen as one way of making sense of oneself and one's own life. And he draws on the words of Oscar Wilde in saying that not only does art imitate life but that life imitates art. We structure our reflections on the events in our lives which seem to us to be significant in determining who we have become. So the story we tell of our lives involves selection (what shall we tell and what shall we leave out?) and it involves reflection. Constructing the narrative of our lives is a complex, culturally shaped set of cognitive and linguistic processes involving the structuring of events, the organisation of memory and the shaping we give to the tale we tell. We shape the tale according to the conventions for telling such tales that exist in our culture.

The poet Michael Rosen chose poetry as a way of structuring some of his stories drawn from his life. In the collection entitled *Carrying the Elephant* he presents events from his life, from his left-wing Jewish upbringing, his trainee days at the BBC, the breakdown of a marriage and the tragic death of his eighteen-year-old son Eddie. Here are some excerpts which illustrate perfectly how selective and reflective this type of autobiography can be.

> My father said the army reached Berlin
> and he was billeted in an empty house. On the
> shelves were the greatest works of German
> Literature – Goethe, Schiller and the rest. And
> Latin. Volume after volume.
>
> (Rosen 2002: 1)

> dear joe, your wild noisy huge brother
> is dead. I couldn't do what my parents did:
> bring two boys, four years apart through the maze.
> I don't know if I'll find my way as well
> as they did, seeing as they lost one
> back near the beginning.
>
> (Rosen 2002: 47)

In the first intensely moving poem Michael Rosen refers to his parents. His father was Harold Rosen who was a storyteller himself and an authority on narrative. In his booklet *Stories and Meanings* he wrote about the power and importance of narrative and included some of his own autobiographical writing. He tells of how he was given the task of storytelling at school and told to select one fiction story and one true and autobiographical one. For his fiction story he selected Oscar Wilde's 'The Happy Prince'. For his true story he told what had happened during a one-hour session at school, and his brief summary of the story went as follows:

> When I was about fourteen some six of us were kept behind in school, the ritual 'detention' of English schools. One boy, a newcomer to the class, set off the fire-extinguisher when the master in charge was out of the classroom. The master, a very ineffectual man, came rushing in and managed to direct the fire extinguisher out of the window, at which point it managed its last feeble spurt.
>
> (Rosen 1984: 36)

What you have here are the bare bones of the story which he developed and which appear as the last chapter in the book. Reading the complete story it becomes clear that the story is fundamentally about something sinister and very troubling and indicative of the time: it is about anti-Semitism.

There are many autobiographies you can read in the forms of story, poetry or diary, but you can also look out for and take notice of the simpler autobiographies children tell or write when they are in your setting. Often they are neither linear nor clear but they are always revealing. Here are some for you to consider.

Here is a beautiful if confused snatch of autobiography written by Alessia:

> The futures of my Mum and my Dad met when they got married, when I was born and when my brother is born. When they meet it's beautiful – like a rainbow. My Grandparents met too when their children were born, Daddy too. Sometimes there are sad things in the future. There are tears. In the middle there are other people's sad and happy futures that they never meet.
>
> (Five and Six Year Old Children of the Fiastri and
> Rodari Preschools 2001: 42)

And here is one written by Loveness, an orphaned six-year-old child living in Swaziland.

> My mum is dead and my dad is dead and my sister is sick and my uncle looks after me. I look after the baby. My uncle goes to work and we have to be outside. He locks the door. The baby cries a lot and it is hot and we get thirsty. My life is sad' (submitted by a student).

And finally one from the host of wonderful stories told and enacted by the children in Paley's kindergarten. You decide if it is autobiography or not.

> Once upon a time there was a mother, a father and two little girls. The father said, 'Get up. Your mother is going to work.' And so they got up and the mother went to work. But the father stayed home. But he wasn't in the room where they was at and they played with the can

opener and their finger got opened. Then the father saw what they had did and he told the mother. And the mother said 'Go to your room'. And they lived happily ever after.

(Paley 1988: 95)

Children deal with the vicissitudes of life in many ways, and one of the most potent of these is the making, telling and sometimes enacting of stories. It is likely that in all of these there will be elements of autobiography because what better to draw on than your own life and your own stories, but there will also be elements of fantasy, humour, tragedy, fear and wonder.

The implications for practice

You will almost certainly already use story and narrative in your class or setting as part of your everyday offer. You may have one or more story sessions or circle times a day, and you may plan these carefully in terms of selecting the books, stories or rhymes, thinking about what, if any, visual aids you will use to draw those children for whom English is an additional language into the meaning. But there is more you can do.

1. *You will want to read to children and tell them stories,* and, more than that, *you will want to find ways of allowing children to create, tell and act out their own stories.* We have seen in this book how Vivian Gussin Paley did that with the children in her kindergarten, and you may enjoy reading the book by Anne Hass Dyson called *Writing Superheroes* (1997). In this book, Dyson analysed work with older children, and her interest was in classes where the teachers were focused on getting the children to know that they were allowed to bring their interests into the classroom. Their interests at the time involved superheroes and other figures drawn from popular culture. The children did this through telling stories. Some practitioners use physical devices to encourage the telling of stories – something like 'the author's chair', for example, where the children can take turns to occupy a particular chair which then allows them to be in charge of the story for the day.

2. As you read stories to the children or listen to the stories they tell, *pay attention to the opportunities within the stories for children to express their feelings.* Sometimes children don't reveal the things that concern, frighten or delight them until they are given permission to do so. Narrative is a wonderful way of doing this. Here is an example, drawn from the work of Paley again. In *The Kindness of Children*, Paley writes about eight-year-old Carrie telling her what she calls a riddle.

Every day you look for someone who likes you and sometimes you think you found a friend, but the next day you have to start again' (a complete and sad story about her struggle to make friends.

(1999: 120–1)

3. You will remember Bruner's insistence that stories and narrative allow children and others to explore universals such as love and hate, fear and anger, right and wrong, jealousy and rivalry and so on. *It is important for you to think carefully about the stories you tell the children and even more carefully about the stories they tell you so that you can identify what serious issues concern them so that you can follow up if necessary.* In the example of Carrie cited above, this is how Paley responded.

> I put an arm around Carrie and wait. She has more to say but once the words are spoken they can no longer be disguised as a riddle ... 'The kids hate me,' she says simply. Four decades of teaching do not lessen the shock of her words ... 'Here's why they hate me so much. The way I talk. And my laugh is stupid. And I never get a joke so I have this dumb look on my face they can't stand ... .'
>
> (Paley 1999: 121)

Paley's ability to tune into the real theme of Carrie's little riddle enabled her to take steps to help the child deal with bullying.

4. Another feature of narrative is that of things not having to be spelled out. If you are asking children to write something factual you need all the details. But narrative allows the writer, the author, to force the reader to do some work. I recently took some children to the theatre. They are children used to television, DVDs, computers, Wiis and other wonders of the technological world. And I was amazed to find that these children were unable to suspend disbelief. When one of the characters pointed to the ceiling of the theatre and said, 'Oh, look at the birds flying overhead', the children did not look up and were amazed that I did. They said, 'We didn't look up because we knew there couldn't be any birds inside the building.' *We need to give children the chance to imagine and to make us imagine with them. So develop your confidence in telling stories as well as reading them.* And when you tell stories use complex language that uses metaphor and simile and that paints pictures in the minds of the children. Of course you need to be sensitive to the need for some children to have visual clues, and this could be one reason for organising some story sessions with visual resources and some without.

5. You will remember that Geertz, the anthropologist, talked of using 'thick description' and meant that different points of view can give a more nuanced view of something. This is particularly true of young children, who will reveal different aspects of themselves and their development to different people or in different contexts. You will know this and in all probability already *ensure that all those involved with the child are involved in contributing to developing a clear picture of how each child is progressing.*

6. Another rather obvious implication is that relating to the expectations you have of the children in your care. It is really important to keep reminding yourself that all children – however young, whatever home they come from, whatever languages they speak – are competent, curious, hypothesis-making, social and interactive beings, eager to communicate and to learn. *Having high expectations means that you will ensure that you offer a curriculum that allows all children to build on their prior experience and to raise and answer questions and to communicate.*

A final word

Bruner, at the grand age of ninety-four, has contributed much to our understanding of how children develop and learn. Much of his work was ground-breaking, and he has influenced students, teachers, policy-makers and others throughout his long life. He has received much recognition and many honours. In 2007, a building in Oxford, where he spent so many productive years, was named in his honour, and at the opening ceremony he lectured on his most recent theories of narrative as a vital learning tool.

He maintained an ethical political stance throughout his life and in all his different roles. As a young man he tried to sign up for the Republicans in the Spanish Civil War and was rejected because of his poor eyesight when he tried to join the military at the start of the Second World War. The events of the 1960s, including the civil-rights movement and the anti-war movement, affected his thinking as it did others of his generation, and he remained something of a rebellious outsider although never a revolutionary.

On a recent visit to the city of Reggio Emilia I visited the Reggio Children Centre in a converted Parmesan-cheese factory dedicated to the memory of Loris Malaguzzi. There, on the wall, alongside photographs of Nelson Mandela, Dario Fo and Howard Gardner, was the smiling face of Jerome Bruner. Beside that, exhibitions of the work of the children in the centres over the years revealing how competent they were, what wonderful questions they raised and answered, how they used everything available to them to express their ideas and thoughts and feelings, all firmly rooted in the culture and context of that particular little town in northern Italy. I remembered how Malaguzzi, when I met him twenty years ago, said that he firmly believed that the foundations laid in the years before formal education would stay with the children and allow them to survive the tedium of formal schooling and emerge as still competent, thinking, expressive, communicative and social beings.

The centre pays homage to the work not only of Malaguzzi but to all of those who supported him: the women in the community, successive political leaders prepared to support and then finance the projects, thinkers and researchers at the university in nearby Bologna and throughout the world, one of whom is Bruner. Within the centre is a permanent although travelling installation called the Atelier Raggio di Luce – the ray of light. This grew out of the experiences of the educationalist in the nurseries and baby–toddler centres in the area, who noticed children's fascination with light and documented the questions they asked and set out to answer. The permanent display explores many aspects of light: how rainbows are made, fluorescence, reflection, shadows, light and water, bending light, refraction, and more. There are four *atelieriste* who work in the installation, and children come in groups to spend time there. There are babies, toddlers, pre-school children and primary-school children, and, just recently, secondary-school children are going. So here we see Bruner's spiral curriculum in action. What the children do and say is being documented and will, eventually, be available as an exhibition or a book.

The *atelieriste* are determined that the approach should be that of promoting the ethos of the hypothesising competent child. They are aware of the fact that formal schooling requires the answering of questions but feel, like Bruner, that education in its broadest sense is about much more than that and that children should have every opportunity to explore anything they encounter that excites them in all possible ways. We have here a marriage between science, logic, aesthetics and feeling. And it is all, as you would expect, deeply rooted in both culture and context. It is this that makes it impossible to 'export' what happens in Reggio Emilia to another place.

Bruner's influence, as we have seen, spread to disciplines other than psychology – his chosen field. His work on narrative was in turn influenced by and influenced the fields of law and medicine and literature as well as the fields of education and early childhood. What he said about narrative sums up his approach and gives us continuing food for thought.

> Storytelling performs the dual cultural functions of making the strange familiar and ourselves private and distinctive. If pupils are encouraged to think about the different outcomes that could have resulted from a set of circumstances, they are demonstrating useability of knowledge about a subject. Rather than just retaining knowledge and facts, they go beyond them to use their imaginations to think about other outcomes, as they don't need the completion of a logical argument to understand a story. This helps them think about the future and it stimulates the teacher too.
>
> (Crace 2007)

In a sense, then, this book has told the story of the life and times and thoughts of an extraordinary man whose life covered almost all of the twentieth century and extends into this twenty-first century. Through an enormous body of work, this man, born blind, became an academic, a teacher, a theorist and a humanitarian and enabled others to see ways in which people learn and teach most effectively. Let us end the book with his own words, written more than a decade ago but still startlingly relevant today.

It is surely the case that schooling is only one small part of how a culture inducts the young into its canonical ways. Indeed, schooling may even be at odds with a culture's other ways of inducting the young into the requirements of communal living. ... What has become increasingly clear ... is that education is not just about conventional school matters like curriculum or standards or testing. What we resolve to do in school only makes sense when considered in the broader context of what the society intends to accomplish through its educational investment in the young. How one conceives of education, we have finally come to recognize, is a function of how one conceives of culture and its aims, professed and otherwise.

(Bruner 1996: ix–x)

Glossary

Note: the key language used by Bruner is indicated in italics.

Abstract

This means thinking about something apart from concrete realities, specific objects or actual instances.

Accommodation

A term used by Piaget which means altering one's existing schemas, or ideas, as a result of new information or new experiences. New schemas may also be developed during this process.

Adaptive responses

These are responses to something in the environment or society.

Affirmative

This means doing something in order to redress something else. Affirmative action can mean ensuring that women or black people or those from another group are given particular consideration in getting or doing something.

Amplification systems

Tools developed within culture: some to enhance action, some to enhance the senses, and some to amplify thought.

Anomaly

Something that doesn't quite fit, that seems odd or strange.

Anthropology

The scientific study of the origin and behaviour of people, including the development of societies and cultures.

Apprentices

A term borrowed from the world of work to describe people who learn alongside more experienced others.

Asili nidi

An Italian term used to describe the settings for the youngest children. Literally means 'nests'.

Assimilation

A term used by Piaget to describe the taking in of new information.

Asymmetric actions	A term used by Bruner to talk about situations where the pair in a dyad are not equals; one, usually the adult, is the agent.
Attention Following (AF)	One of the ways of interaction where the caregiver follows the child's focus of attention.
Attention-mapping hypothesis	Tomasello used this phrase to describe the child and caregiver engaging in an action with shared attention.
Attention switching	One of the ways of interaction where the caregiver switches the child's focus of attention to theirs.
Biological needs	The needs of human infants for food, drink, warmth, shelter and other essentials for growth and development.
Buffered	Bruner used the term to mean protected.
Causation	The understanding of cause and effect.
Cerebral development	The growth and development of the brain and of thinking.
Codes	Bernstein talked of linguistic codes which differed according to context, culture and experience.
Cognition	A term referring to the mental processes involved in gaining knowledge and understanding, including thinking, knowing, remembering, judging and problem-solving. These are higher-level functions of the brain and encompass language, imagination, perception and planning.
Cognitive development	Also known as intellectual or mental development – the processes by which we come to be able to know and to understand.
Cognitive map/mental map	A cognitive map is a mental representation of the layout of one's environment For example, when a friend asks you for directions to your house, you are able to create an image in your mind of the roads, places to turn, landmarks, etc., along the way to your house from your friend's starting point. This representation is the cognitive map.
Cognitive science	The interdisciplinary study of mind or the study of thought. It embraces multiple research disciplines, including psychology, artificial intelligence, philosophy, neuroscience, linguistics, anthropology, sociology and biology.

Communication	The sharing of meaning between animals or people.
Communities of practice	Groups of people who share a common domain or area of interest and expertise. For our purposes, children learning together may be seen as a community of practice.
Compensatory	To make up for a perceived deficit.
Competent	The common-sense definition would be 'able'. A competent infant is one equipped to learn.
Conditioned reflex	A reflex in which the response (e.g., the secretion of saliva in a dog) is caused by a secondary stimulus (e.g., the ringing of a bell) repeatedly associated with the primary stimulus (e.g., the sight of meat).
Constrained	Limited or restricted by something.
Constraints tenet	One of Bruner's four possible tenets. In all thinking, according to Bruner, there are constraints coming both from the child's own experience and being imposed by the culture.
Constructivism	A philosophy of learning founded on the idea that by reflecting on our experiences we construct our own understanding of the world in which we live. Each of us generates our own 'rules' and 'mental models', which we use to make sense of our experiences. Learning, therefore, is simply the process of adjusting our mental models to accommodate new experiences.
Constructivist tenet	Another tenet and here Bruner reminds us that meaning is not found but constructed or made.
Context	This means where something takes place and the 'where' does not only refer to place but more widely to things like with whom, in what circumstances, what setting and so on.
Core member	Someone who is fully accepted by other members of a community of practice.
Cultural deprivation	A view which suggests that there is something lacking within cultures or groups. It views languages other than English as not as good as English, for example.
Cultural transmission	The process of passing on the thoughts, ideas, concepts, values, beliefs and principles of a culture from one generation to the next.

Culture	This is a word which can be defined in many ways. Here is one simple definition which is a good starting place. Culture can be summarised as the totality of socially transmitted behaviour patterns, arts, beliefs, institutions and all other products of human work and thought.
Culture-free	Something that is beyond culture although difficult to find an example. Education and pedagogy are certainly not culture-free.
Curriculum	This is an everyday word but it can be used in several senses. For our purposes we can define a curriculum as a programme of learning which refers to what is to be learned, by whom, for how long and according to what style of teaching and learning.
Deep structure	This was a term used by Chomsky to describe his notional innate capacity for humans to be able to process the rules of language.
Deficit	Something wrong or missing.
Deixis	A technical linguistic term to mean where the meaning of certain words is dependent on the context.
Denotational	Something that indicates or refers to.
Development of mind	We can define this as the processes by which human beings become able to think, reason, pose and solve problems, use language and other symbolic systems and so on.
Developmental diaries	Records of development usually made by parents.
Deviser	Someone or something that creates or invents something.
Dialogic	Ways of teaching and learning where the learner plays an active role and engages in questioning rather than being passive and answering questions.
Domain	An area or matter of interest.
Dyad	This is a pair of people. It is used in our context to describe the interaction between the mother or caregiver and the child.
Egocentrically	From the point of view of the person his- or herself.
Elaborated code	Bernstein described the code of speech of middle-class English people as being elaborated, by which he meant able to be used without the need for a shared context.

Enactive	*One of Bruner's terms describing the first of his representation stages where the child uses movement and the senses.*
Endemic	Common or prevalent.
Endowments	Abilities or capacities.
Epistemology	The study of the nature of knowledge.
Equilibrium	One of Piaget's terms whose meaning is not clear. It means balance, which he says is the aim of learning.
Explicit	Something that is obvious and evident. It means the opposite of implicit.
Folk pedagogy	A term used by Bruner to talk about what ordinary or lay people think about teaching.
Formal education	This is when children enter statutory education and is often to used to suggest that what is required of the learner is the ability to think abstractly – to reason and be logical and no longer require direct hands-on experience.
Formats	*A key concept of Bruner's which describes the ways in which adults in particular are able to scaffold the learning of children through repeated actions or routines.*
Goal structure	In all interactions there is the possibility of some sort of reward or goal.
Goal-directed behaviour	Behaviour directed towards a goal – reaching for a toy, for example.
Grammar	The rules binding language together.
Hard-wired	This means inborn or innate.
Hominids	Apes.
Homophones	Words that sound the same – e.g., 'herd' and 'heard', 'by' and 'buy' and so on.
Hunter-gatherer groups	Groups of people who live by hunting and gathering food.
Iconic	*The second of Bruner's stages of representation: the use of images and pictures.*
Idealised	The image of an ideal person or family or parent or child. This is, by definition, biased in favour of the group of the person holding this view.
Implicit	Something that is not evident but has to be worked out or guessed at.
Induct	To draw someone into something.
Initial cognitive endowment	The ability to learn that someone is born with.
Innate	Born with.

Intention	Purpose or goal. For Bruner the life of the infant was characterised by intentional or purposeful behaviours.
Interaction	Exchanges between two or more people.
Interactional tenet	Another of Bruner's tenets and here the meaning is clear. Learning is social and people learn with and through others.
Interdisciplinary	This is where more than one discipline is involved in considering an issue. By a discipline we are thinking of areas of study and thinking. So interdisciplinary in terms of the work of Bruner is considering something from the point of view of psychology, anthropology or linguistics and so on.
Internal	Internal has an everyday meaning of 'inside'. In this context it often refers to what takes place unseen, within the brain of the learner.
Interpretive social sciences	This is a difficult term to explain. What it means is those social sciences that are interested in explaining through methods such as observation or interview rather than measuring or testing.
Intersubjectivity	For our purposes this means the shared meanings constructed by people in their interactions with each other and used as an everyday resource to interpret the meaning of elements of social and cultural life.
Intonation patterns	The particular patterns of sounds produced by fluent speakers of a language. They may vary from person to person, from role to role and according to things such as social class.
Joint attention	Where people are paying attention to the same thing.
Joint intention	Where people are working towards the same goal or purpose.
Labile	Easily bored or fatigued.
Language	A way of communicating using sounds or other mutually recognisable symbolic systems such as writing.
Language acquisition	The way in which the human infant begins to acquire and use language in its broadest sense, which includes all forms of communication (gesture, intonation, eye-pointing as well as speech).

Language Acquisition Device (LAD)	The term introduced by Chomsky to describe his hypothesised innate mental faculty with which human infants are born and that enables them to construct and internalise the grammar of their native language on the basis of the limited and fragmentary language input to which they are exposed.
Language Acquisition Support System (LASS)	*The term used by Bruner to enhance Chomsky's LAD and to ensure that any analysis of language acquisition took place within the context of family and other support contexts.*
Learning	At its most basic this means acquiring knowledge and skills although it should apply also to beliefs, values, principles, concepts, ideas and so on.

- Prior learning What the learner has already learned.

Legitimate peripheral participation	This is where the learner is at the initial stages of becoming part of the group and is accepted and not isolated.
Logic	Reasoning.
Logical thinking	Reasoning that is logical and consistent.
Linguistic	To do with language.

- Prelinguistic Before the acquisition of language, although the term is often in dispute.

Meaning	Understanding or comprehending: to make meaning means to make sense of.
Means–end readiness	*An expression used particularly by Bruner and referring to the potential to make an action in order to achieve a goal.*
Mechanistic	Tending to explain phenomena only by reference to physical or biological causes.

- Mechanistic view of language learning Explaining language acquisition with reference to biology rather than to culture and interaction

Mediation	The word sometimes means the process of working towards a goal but in the sense in which Vygotsky and Bruner used the term it means the process used by a more experienced learner to assist another learner.

Mind	Means that which is responsible for one's thoughts and feelings; the seat of the faculty of reason.
Moderator	Something that limits or eases something.
Narrative	*Another word for storytelling and important for Bruner as the way in which we make sense of our experience.*
Nativism	A term used more frequently in the USA and referring to the tendency to place the needs of the 'native' group over those of others.
Niche	This comes from the French word for 'nest' and means a place or position which is particular to a person or a thought.
Non-nutritive sucking	Sucking for reasons other than obtaining food or other sustenance.
Novel utterance	A word used by Chomsky to describe the things that young children say that can never have been heard by them from a fluent speaker of the language. Novel, here, means new.
Object highlighting	*A phrase used by Bruner to explain what a caregiver does when drawing the child's attention to an object.*
Object play formats	*Also used by Bruner to indicate the routines around learning the names of objects.*
Ordered	Means systematic.
Paradigmatic	Something that can be a model.
Pedagogy	The art or science of teaching.
Peripheral member	Someone who is not fully accepted as a member of a group.
Perspective tenet	One of Bruner's tenets, this one emphasising how learners become able to take on the views and ideas of others.
Place holder	A phrase used by Bruner to describe how words come to be used in place of objects – allowing the child to move towards the use of symbols.
Play	Can be defined in many ways. For our purposes it is what children do when they identify something that interests them and find ways to express their ideas, thoughts or feelings. The essence of play is that it is self-chosen and purposeful.
Political	Can be used in many senses. In this book Bruner is described as someone who is political in the sense that he often considered issues like power and agency.
Positive social response	A response that is pleasing to those receiving it – a smile or a kind remark, for example.

Practice	What one does.
Predispose	Be equipped to do or achieve something.
Predetermined goals	These are goals or outcomes decided before the activity and imposed on the learner. They are often regarded as inappropriate for younger children who are setting their own goals in their search for meaning.
Protagonist	The one playing the leading role in the drama.
Protonarrative	The first or earliest stories.
Psycholinguistic	Psycholinguistics or the psychology of language is the study of the psychological and neurobiological factors that enable humans to acquire, use, comprehend and produce language. You will recognise that it pays no attention to the social, the cultural or the contextual.
Psychology	Dictionary definitions say psychology is the study of the mind and of individual development.
Reciprocal respect	How Bruner described the ethos of the city of Reggio Emilia. It means how children are respected and in return show respect, how educators are respected and in return show respect, and how parents and carers are respected and in return show respect.
Reference or naming	*It literally means drawing attention to something and this is helpful in making us always aware that naming involves interaction and shared attention.*
Reference system	A system for arranging and classifying – an essential cognitive tool for children to develop.
Referential	A way of referring to something – words, pointing, looking and so on.
Reflexes	This is an involuntary and nearly instantaneous movement in response to a stimulus.
Reinforcer	Something that ensures that something will happen again.
Reinforcement	Means ensuring that something will be repeated.
Repository	A storage place.
Request	*Bruner's term for asking a question or asking for help or support.*
Request for action	Where the child may be asked to do something.

Request for information	Where the child is asked why he or she is doing something.
Restricted code	Bernstein's code used to describe the language used by people sharing a reference or a context.
Routinised	*To make something common through repetition.*
Rule-bound	*Something that is tied together by rules. For Bruner this applied to communication systems such as language.*
Scarification	The practice of making scars as part of rituals around coming of age.
Scaffolding	*The word used by Bruner to say what adults do to support learning when they offer the child help, step by step, from dependence on help to independence.*
Schemas	A term used by Piaget to explain the often observed repeated patterns of behaviour.
Self-initiated	More commonly referred to as self-chosen or self-selected it also means the one starting an action or a process.
Sensory processing	This is defined as the method the nervous system uses to receive, organise and understand sensory input.
Shared collective intentionality	This is where the child becomes inducted into collective features of his or her culture – things like values and beliefs.
Social rituals	These are the habits and customs features of social groups and can refer to things such as the rules about what is regarded as appropriate behaviour.
Social pedagogues	People employed with the specific task of promoting the child's learning and development.
Spiral curriculum	*One of Bruner's best-known theories insisting that something can be taught to a child at any age as long as the style of teaching and support is matched to the child's capacities at the time.*
Supportive action	This means help. The child asks the adult for help.
Surface structure	A term used by Chomsky to explain the features of language that are apparent, such as the words.
Symbolic	*The third of Bruner's representational stages, where the learner is able to use abstract systems such as symbols.*
Symboliser	Something that stands for something else.

Syntactic	This means to do with grammar or the rules that bind a language together.
Systematic	Something that is characterised by order and planning.
Systematicity	This term, favoured by Bruner, means the tendency to be systematic and applies particularly to language.
Thick description	A term used by Geertz to mean building up a picture by using the interpretations of not just one person but many.
Transactionality	A difficult term to define, but it means something relating to an exchange or agreement between two parties. I would suggest that it means interaction.
Translocational	To do with something or someone being moved physically in some way. It is used by Bruner to discuss the child's request for help.
Universal grammar	A theory of linguistics which states that the principles of grammar are shared by all languages and are innate to humans and which attempts to explain language acquisition in general. It proposes a set of rules intended to explain language acquisition in child development.
Word order	The rules about how sentences can be made within a particular language.
Zone of proximal development	Vygotsky's notional gap between what the child could to unaided and what the child might do with help. It is this notional gap that may be bridged by the learning being scaffolded.

Bibliography

Addessi, A. (2009) 'The Musical Dimension of Daily Routine with under-Four Children During Diaper Change, Bedtime and Free-Play', *Early Child Development and Care*, 179 (6): 747–68.

Axline, V. (1964) *Dibs: In Search of Self – Personality Development in Play Therapy*, Harmondsworth: Penguin.

Barron, I (2009) 'Illegitimate Participation? A Group of Young Minority Ethnic Children's Experiences of Early Childhood Education', *Pedagogy, Culture and Society*, 17 (3): 341–54.

Bernhard, J. E. (2004) 'Behaviour and Misbehaviour of Latino Children in a Time of Zero Tolerance: Mothers' Views', *Early Years*, 24 (1): 49–62.

Bernstein, B. (1971) *Class, Codes and Control*, vol. I, London: Paladin.

Bower, T. G. R. (1979) *A Primer of Infant Development*, San Francisco, Calif.: W. H. Freeman & Co. Ltd.

Brazelton, T. A. (1995) *The Neonatal Behavioral Assessment Scale*, Cambridge: Mac Keith Press.

Brooker, L. (2002) *Starting School: Young Children Learning Cultures*, Buckingham and Philadelphia, Pa.: Open University Press.

Brown, R. (1973) *A First Language*, Cambridge: Cambridge University Press.

Bruner, J. S. (1957) 'Going Beyond the Information Given', in J. S. Bruner, E. Brunswik, L. Festinger, F. Heider, K. F. Muenzinger, C. E. Osgood and D. Rapaport, (eds), *Contemporary Approaches to Cognition*, Cambridge, Mass.: Harvard University Press, pp. 41–69. Reprinted in J. S. Bruner (1973) *Beyond the Information Given*, New York: Norton, pp. 218–38.

——(1966a) *The Growth of Mind*, Newton, Mass.: American Psychological Association.

——(1966b) *Towards a Theory of Instruction*, Cambridge, Mass.: Harvard University Press.

——(1983a) *In Search of Mind: Essays in Autobiography*, Cambridge, New York and Philadelphia, Pa.: Harper Colophon.

——(1983b) *Child's Talk: Learning to Use Language*, Oxford: Oxford University Press.

——(1990) *Acts of Meaning*, Cambridge, Mass: Harvard University Press.

——(1996) *The Culture of Education*, Cambridge, Mass.: Harvard University Press.

——(2002) *Making Stories: Law, Literature, Life*, Cambridge, Mass.: Harvard University Press.

——(2004) 'Reggio: A City of Courtesy, Curiosity and Imagination', *Children in Europe*, 6: 27.

Bruner, J. S. and Lucariello, J. (1989) 'Monologues as Narrative Recreation of the World', in K. Nelson (ed.), *Narratives from the Crib*, Cambridge, Mass.: Harvard University Press, pp. 73–97.

Cameron, C. (2007) 'Social Pedagogy and the Children's Workforce', available online at http://www.communitycare.co.uk/articles/2007/08/08/105392/social-pedagogy-and-the-childrens-workforce.html (accessed 19 October 2010).

Cavallini, I. F. (2008) *We Write Shapes That Look Like a Book*, Reggio Emilia: Reggio Children Coriandoli.

Crace, J. (2007) 'Jerome Bruner: The Lesson of the Story', interview in *The Guardian*, 27 March.

Dunn, J. (1988) *The Beginnings of Social Understanding*, Oxford: Blackwell.

Dyson, A. H. (1997) *Writing Superheroes: Contemporary Childhood, Popular Culture and Classroom Literacy*, New York: Teachers College Press.

Ebrahim, Hasina Banu (2008) 'Situated Ethics: Possibilities for Young Children As Research Participants in the South African Context', *Early Child Development and Care*, 1–10.

Emiliani, F. (2002) *Il Bambino Nella Vita Quotidiana (The Child in Everyday Life)*, Rome: Carocci.

Five- and Six-Year Old Children of the Fiastri and Rodari Preschools (2001) *The Future Is a Lovely Day*, Reggio Emilia: Reggio Children.

Francis, H. (1983) 'How Do Children Learn to Say What They Mean?' *Early Childhood Development and Care*, 11: 3–18.

Geertz, C. (1973) *The Interpretation of Cultures: Selected Essays*, New York: Basic Books.

Gillen, J. C. (2007) '"A Day in the Life": Advancing a Methodology for the Cultural Study of Development and Learning in Early Childhood', *Early Child Development and Care*, 177 (2): 207–18.

Gopnik, A. M., Meltzoff, A. N. and Kuhl, P. K. (1999) *The Scientist in the Crib: What Early Learning Tells Us About the Mind*, New York: HarperCollins.

Guadalupe San Miguel, J. (1987) *'Let All of Them Take Heed': Mexican Americans and the Campaign for Educational Equality in Texas*, Austin, Tex.: University of Texas Press.

Inghilleri, M. (2002) 'Britton and Bernstein on Vygotsky: Divergent Views on Mind and Language in the Pedagogic Context', *Pedagogy, Culture and Society*, 10 (3): 467–82.

Karmiloff-Smith, A. (1994) *Baby It's You: A Unique Insight into the First Three Years of the Developing Baby*, London: Random House.

Kenner, C. (2010) 'Learning about Writing through Bilingual Peer Teaching', in S. Smidt (ed.), *Key Issues in Early Years Education*, London and New York: Routledge, pp. 66–72.

Kyriacou, C. I. (2009) 'Social Pedagogy and the Teacher: England and Norway Compared', *Pedagogy, Culture and Society*, 17 (1): 75–87.

Lee, H. (1960) *To Kill a Mockingbird*, London: Pan Books.

Macrory, G. (2007) 'Constructing Language: Evidence from a French–English Bilingual Child', *Early Child Development and Care*, 177 (6 and 7): 781–92.

McDonagh, J. A. and McDonagh, S. (1999) 'Learning to Talk, Talking to Learn', in J. Marsh and E. Hallet (eds), *Desirable Literacies*, London: Paul Chapman, pp. 1–17.

Mattingly, C. L., Lutkehaus, N. C. and Throop, C. J. (2008) 'Bruner's Search for Meaning: A Conversation Between Psychology and Anthropology', *Ethos*, 6 (1): 1–28.

Paley, V. G. (1988) *Bad Guys Don't Have Birthdays: Fantasy Play at Four*, Chicago, Ill.: University of Chicago Press.

——(1999) *The Kindness of Children*, Cambridge, Mass.: Harvard University Press.

Petrie, P. (2005) 'Schools and Support Staff', *Support for Learning*, 20 (4): 176–80.

Pinker, S. (1994) *The Language Instinct.* London: Penguin.

Reggio Tutta (2001) *Reggio Tutta: A guide to the city by the children*, Reggio Emilia: Reggio children.

Rosen, H. (1984) *Stories and Meanings*, Kettering: Nate Papers in Education.

Rosen, M. (2002) *Carrying the Elephant: A Memoir of Love and Loss*, London: Penguin.

Roy, A. (1998) *The God of Small Things*, London: Flamingo.

Rudd, L. D. (2008) 'Does Improving Joint Attention in Low-Quality Child-Care Enhance Language Development?' *Early Child Development and Care*, 178 (3): 315–38.

Saxon, T. F. and Reilly, J. (1998) 'Language Competence and Joint Attention in Mother–Toddler Dyads', *Early Childhood Development and Care*, 142: 33–42.

Smidt, S. (2009) *Introducing Vygotsky: A Guide for Practitioners and Students in Early Years Education*, London and New York: Routledge.

Snow, C. (1977) 'The Development of Conversation between Mothers and Babies', *Journal of Child Language*, 4: 1–22.

Stern, D. H. (1982) 'Interpersonal Communication: The Attunement of Affected States by Means of Intermodal Fluency', paper presented at the International Conference on Infancy Studies, Austin, Texas, March.

Sylva, K. E.-B. (2004) *The Effective Provision of Pre-School Education (EPPE) Project: Findings from Pre-School to End of Key Stage 1*, London: Sure Start.

Tallis, R. (2010) *Michelangelo's Finger: An Exploration of Everyday Transcendence*, London: Atlantic Books.

Tomasello, M. A. and Rakoczy, H. (1992) 'The Social Bases of Language Acquisition', *Social Development*, 1: 67–87.

——(1999) *The Cultural Origins of Human Cognition*, Cambridge, Mass: Harvard University Press.

——(2003) 'What Makes Human Cognition Unique? From Individual to Shared to Collective Intentionality', *Mind and Language*, 18 (2): 121–47.

Wells, G. (1981) *Learning through Interaction: The Study of Language Development*, Cambridge: Cambridge University Press.

Wenger, E. (1998) *Communities of Practice: Learning, Meaning, and Identity*, Cambridge: Cambridge University Press.

Williams, A. (2004) 'Playing School in Mulitethnic London', in S. L. E. Gregory (ed.), *Many Pathways to Literacy*, London and New York: RoutledgeFalmer, pp. 52–65.

Index